Table of Contents

1 Crime and Criminology

LEARNING OBJECTIVES

After mastering the content of this chapter, a student should be able to:

1. Understand what is meant by the "field of criminology."
2. Know the historical context of criminology.
3. Recognize the differences between the various schools of criminological thought.
4. Discuss the concept of positivism.
5. Understand the various elements of the criminological enterprise.
6. Discuss how criminologists define crime.
7. Recognize the concepts of criminal law.
8. Show how the criminal law is undergoing change.
9. Discuss ethical issues in criminology.
10. Understand international crime trends.
11. Describe the various criminal defenses.

KEY WORDS AND DEFINITIONS

Criminology - The scientific study of the nature, extent, cause, and control of crime. p. 2

Criminal Justice – The agencies of social control that handle criminal offenders. p. 2

Interdisciplinary – Involving two or more academic fields. p. 2

Utilitarianism - The view that people's behavior is motivated by the pursuit of pleasure and the avoidance of pain. p. 4

Classical criminology - The theoretical perspective suggesting that (1) people have free will to choose criminal or conventional behaviors; (2) people choose to commit crime for reasons of greed or personal need; and (3) crime can be controlled only by the fear of criminal sanctions. p. 3

Positivism - The branch of social science that uses the scientific method of the natural sciences and suggests that human behavior is a product of social, biological, psychological, or economic forces. p. 3

Scientific method - Using verifiable principles and procedures for the systematic acquisition of knowledge. p. 3

Biosocial theory - Approach to criminology that focuses on the interaction between biological and social factors as they relate to crime. p. 4

Sociological criminology - Approach to criminology, based on the work of Quertelet and Durkheim that focuses on the relationship between social factors and crime. p. 4

Anomie - A lack of norms or clear social standards. Because of rapidly shifting moral values, the individual has few guides to what is socially acceptable. p. 5

Chicago School - Group of urban sociologists who studied the relationship between environmental conditions and crime. p. 5

Socialization - Process of human development and enculturation. Socialization is influenced by key social processes and institutions. p. 5

Conflict theory - The view that human behavior is shaped by interpersonal conflict and that those who maintain social power will use it to further their own ends. p. 5

Critical criminology - The view that crime is a product of the capitalist system. p. 5

Developmental theory – The view that criminality is a dynamic process influenced by social experiences as well as individual characteristics. p. 6

Rational choice theory - The view that crime is a function of a decision-making process in which the potential offender weighs the potential costs and benefits of an illegal act. p. 6

Social structure theory - The view that disadvantaged economic class position is a primary cause of crime. p. 7

Trait theory – The view that criminality is a product of abnormal biological or psychological traits. p. 6

Social process theory – The view that criminality is a function of people's interactions with various organizations, institutions, and processes in society. p. 7

Valid - Actually measuring what one intends to measure; relevant. p. 8

Reliable - Producing consistent results from one measurement to another. p. 8

Ex post facto law - A law applied retroactively to punish acts that were not crimes before its passage, or that raises the grade of an offense, or that renders an act punishable in a more severe manner than it was when committed. p. 9

White-collar crime - Illegal acts that capitalize on a person's status in the marketplace. White-collar crimes may include theft, embezzlement, fraud, market manipulation, restraint of trade, and false advertising. p. 10

Penology – Area of criminology that focuses on the correction and control of criminal offenders. p. 11

Rehabilitation - Treatment of criminal offenders aimed at preventing future criminal behavior. p. 11

Capital punishment - The execution of criminal offenders; the death penalty. p. 11

Mandatory sentences - A statutory requirement that a certain penalty shall be carried out in all cases of conviction for a specified offense or series of offenses. p. 11

Victimology - The study of the victim's role in criminal events. p. 12

Deviance - Behavior that departs from the social norm but is not necessarily criminal. p. 12

Crime - An act, deemed socially harmful or dangerous, that is specifically defined, prohibited, and punished under the criminal law. p. 12

Decriminalize – Having criminal penalties reduced rather than eliminated. p. 13

Consensus view - The belief that the majority of citizens in a society share common values and agree on what behaviors should be defined as criminal. p. 14

Criminal law - The written code that defines crimes and their punishments. p. 14

Conflict view - The belief that criminal behavior is defined by those in a position of power to protect and advance their own self-interest. p. 14

Interactionist view - The belief that those with social power are able to impose their values on society as a whole, and these values then define criminal behavior. p. 15

Code of Hammurabi - The first written criminal code, developed in Babylonia about 2000 B.C. p. 16

Mosaic Code - The laws of the ancient Israelites, found in the Old Testament of the Judeo-Christian Bible. p. 16

Precedent - A rule derived from previous judicial decisions and applied to future cases; the basis of common law. p. 16

Common law - Early English law, developed by judges, which became the standardized law of the land in England and eventually formed the basis of the criminal law in the United States. p. 16

Statutory crimes - Crimes defined by legislative bodies in response to changing social conditions, public opinion, and custom. p. 16

Felony - A serious offense that carries a penalty of imprisonment, usually for one year or more, and may entail loss of political rights. p. 16

Misdemeanor - A minor crime usually punished by a short jail term and/or a fine. p. 16

Appellate court - Court that reviews trial court procedures to determine whether they have complied with accepted rules and constitutional doctrines. p. 18

CHAPTER SUMMARY

Criminology is the scientific approach to the study of criminal behavior and society's reaction to law violations and violators. It is essentially an interdisciplinary field; many of its practitioners were originally trained as sociologists, psychologists, economists, political scientists, historians, and natural scientists. Criminology has a rich history, with roots in the utilitarian philosophy of Beccaria (crime is the result of free will), the biological positivism of Lombroso (crime is the result of a biological trait), the social theory of Durkheim (crime is primarily a product social forces) and the political philosophy of Marx (crime is a by-product of capitalism).

When they define crime, criminologists typically hold one of three perspectives: the consensus view, the conflict view, or the interactionist view. The consensus view holds that criminal behavior is defined by laws that reflect the values and morals of a majority of citizens. The conflict view states that criminal behavior is defined in such a way that economically powerful groups can retain their control over society. The interactionist view portrays criminal behavior as a relativistic, constantly changing concept that reflects society's current moral values. According to the interactionist view, behavior is labeled as criminal by those in power; criminals are people society chooses to label as outsiders or deviants.

Regardless of their perspective or training, all criminologists seek to study crime and criminal behavior. Measuring criminological enterprises includes subareas such as criminal statistics, the sociology of law, theory construction, criminal behavior systems, penology, and victimology. Criminologists strive to make their research measurements valid and reliable. Criminologists also develop theories of crime causation in addition to attempting to understand and describe criminal behavior. For example, it was the criminologist Edwin Sutherland who developed the term white-collar crime to describe economic crime by the wealthy.

The criminal law is a set of rules that specify the behaviors society has outlawed. The criminal law serves several important purposes: It represents public opinion and moral values, it enforces social controls, it deters criminal behavior and wrongdoing, it punishes transgressors, it creates equity, and it banishes private retribution. While the Code of Hammurabi (1792-1750 B.C.) is the earliest recognized form of criminal law, the criminal law used in U.S. jurisdictions traces its origin to the English common law. In the U.S. legal system, lawmakers have codified common-law crimes into state and federal penal codes. The criminal law is undergoing constant reform. Some acts are being decriminalized—their penalties are being reduced—while penalties for others are becoming more severe. Felonies are the more serious crimes such as rape and murder; misdemeanors include lesser offenses such as shoplifting and disturbing the peace. Appellate courts review lower court decisions in these cases.

CHAPTER OUTLINE

I. A Brief History of Criminology
    A. Classical Criminology
        1. Utilitarianism
        2. Free Will
    B. Positivist Criminology
        1. Scientific Method
        2. Biological Determinism
    C. Sociological Criminology
        1. Anomie
        2. Chicago School
        3. Socialization
    D. Conflict Criminology
        1. Karl Marx
        2. Critical criminology
    E. Developmental Criminology
    F. Contemporary Criminology
        1. Rational choice theory
        2. Trait Theory
        3. Social Structure Theory
        4. Social Process Theory

II. What Criminologists Do: The Field of Criminology
   A. Criminal Statistics/Crime Measurement
      1. Validity
      2. Reliability
   B. Sociology of Law
   C. Developing Theories of Crime Causation
   D. Understanding and Describing Criminal Behavior
   E. Penology
      1. Rehabilitation
      2. Capital Punishment
      3. Mandatory Sentences
   F. Victimology

III. Deviant or Criminal? How Criminologists Define Crime
   A. Deviance
   B. Becoming Deviant
   C. The Concept of Crime
   D. The Consensus View of Crime
   E. The Conflict View of Crime
   F. The Interactionist View of Crime
   G. A Definition of Crime

IV. Crime and the Criminal Law
   A. Common Law
      1. Precedent
      2. Statutory Crimes
   B. Contemporary Criminal Law
      1. Felony
      2. Misdemeanor
   C. The Evolution of Criminal Law

V. Ethical Issues in Criminology: Who, What and How to Study

CRITICAL THINKING QUESTIONS

1. Criminology is an interdisciplinary science. List several of the reasons you believe people commit crime. Into what disciplines would your "causes" fit?

2. Classical criminologists suggest that "the punishment fit the crime." How would you apply this way of thinking to criminal behaviors such as computer hacking and public drunkenness?

3. Research several international crime trends and apply the theory you think best explains the crime trend.

4. If you were a "moral entrepreneur" what laws would you like to see enforced? Would you support laws against pornography, prostitution and drugs?

CHAPTER REVIEW QUESTIONS

Multiple Choice

1. Criminology is _____ science.
   a. a unidisciplinary
   b. an interdisciplinary
   c. a pure
   d. primarily a psychological

2. Lombroso's early scientific work was called
   a. atavism.
   b. biological determinism.
   c. biosocial theory.
   d. rational anomie theory.

3. The scientific method is a main element of _____ criminology.
   a. Classical
   b. Utilitarian
   c. Positivist
   d. Atavist

4. Norm and role confusion resulting from structural changes in society is called
   a. anomie.
   b. atavism.
   c. phrenology.
   d. penology.

5. Quertelet and Durkheim were the pioneering founders of _____ criminology.
   a. biological
   b. sociological
   c. classical
   d. positivist

6. Sutherland linked criminality to the failure of
   a. socialization.
   b. biological treatments.
   c. masculinity.
   d. capitalism.

7. The view that human behavior is shaped by interpersonal conflict and that those in power will use it to further their own ends is the _____ perspective.
   a. Positivism
   b. Socialization
   c. Classical
   d. Conflict

8. _____ refers to actually measuring what one intended to.
   a. Validity
   b. Responsibility
   c. Legitimacy
   d. Reliability

9. When research produces consistent results from one measurement to another, it is said to be
   a. valid.
   b. responsible.
   c. legitimate.
   d. reliable.

10. Crimes are behaviors that all elements of society consider to be repugnant according to _____.
    a. the consensus view of crime
    b. the conflict view of crime
    c. the interactionist view of crime
    d. the specious view of crime

11. According to which view of crime does the definition of crime reflect the preferences and opinions of people who hold social power in a particular legal jurisdiction?
    a. the consensus view of crime
    b. the conflict view of crime
    c. the interactionist view of crime
    d. the specious view of crime

12. Which view of crime depicts society as a collection of diverse groups who are in constant and continuing conflict?
    a. the consensus view of crime
    b. the conflict view of crime
    c. the interactionist view of crime
    d. the specious view of crime

13. The area of _____ focuses on studying the agencies of social control that handle criminal offenders.
    a. institutionalism
    b. management
    c. criminal justice
    d. social organization

14. Positivist criminology is the application of _____ to the study of human behavior.
    a. the scientific method
    b. humanism
    c. utilitarianism
    d. hedonism

15. The most commonly represented discipline in criminology is
    a. political science.
    b. sociology.
    c. criminal justice.
    d. economics.

16. A _____ is a serious criminal offense that carries a penalty of imprisonment for one year or more.
    a. felony
    b. misdemeanor
    c. statutory offense
    d. traffic citation

17. Karl Marx discussed how crime is caused by
    a. socialism.
    b. communism.
    c. capitalism.
    d. utilitarianism.

18. _____ is the process of discouraging criminal behavior through the fear of punishment.
    a. Victimology
    b. Peacemaking
    c. Rehabilitation
    d. Deterrence

19. Courts that review trial court procedures are called
    a. peoples courts.
    b. appellate courts.
    c. administrative courts.
    d. superior courts.

20. The roots of criminology come from each of the following EXCEPT
    a. the utilitarian philosophy of Beccaria.
    b. the biological positivism of Lombroso.
    c. the social theory of Durkheim.
    d. the political philosophy of Mahatma Gandhi.

21. During the Middle Ages, people who violated social norms or religious practices were punished by means of
    a. brandings.
    b. long prison sentences.
    c. large fines.
    d. Intensive probation.

22. Shaw and McKay did their groundbreaking study of social ecology in which city?
    a. Detroit
    b. Seattle
    c. Chicago School
    d. New York

23. _____ indicts the economic system as producing the conditions that support high crime rates and is founded on Marxist theory.
    a. Rational choice theory
    b. Biosocial criminology
    c. Developmental theory
    d. Critical criminology

24. Theory construction focuses on
    a. determining the origin of law.
    b. evaluating scientific methods.
    c. predicting individual behavior.
    d. gathering valid crime data.

25. _____ are laws applied retroactively to punish behavior that was not a crime prior to passage of the law.
    a. Retroactive law.
    b. Ex post facto law.
    c. Mandatory law.
    d. Indeterminate law.

26. The Enron case offers an example of _____ crime.
    a. white-collar
    b. ex post facto
    c. mandatory
    d. blue line

27. The area of criminology that focuses on the correction and control of known criminal offenders is called
    a. recidivism.
    b. penology.
    c. victimology.
    d. deviance.

28. Victimology includes which of the following areas of interest?
    a. calculating probabilities of victimization risk
    b. predicting victim biological traits
    c. rehabilitating criminals through victim impact statements
    d. mandating criminal behavior modification

29. _____ occurs when criminal penalties are reduced rather than eliminated.
    a. Deviance
    b. Delinquency
    c. Deliberation
    d. Decriminalization

30. _____ is the basis of Judeo-Christian and the U.S. system.
    a. The Code of Hammurabi
    b. The Magna Carta
    c. The Mosaic Code
    d. The United Nations Charter

True/False

1. T / F According to the classical school, in order for punishment to be effective, it must be swift, certain and severe.

2. T / F The founder of the positivist school was Cesare Beccaria.

3. T / F Positivists would challenge a concept such as the "soul" because it cannot be verified by the scientific method.

4. T / F Positivists believe that deviant behavior is a product of free will of the individual.

5. T / F The consensus view claims the law is a tool of the ruling class.

6. T / F Statutory crimes are also known as mala in se crimes.

7. T / F The Mosaic Code contains the laws of the ancient Israelites, found in the Old Testament of the Judeo-Christian Bible.

8. T / F Classical criminology suggests that people choose to commit crime for reasons of greed or personal need.

9. T / F The Chicago School sociologists argued that crime was a function of personal traits or characteristics.

10. T / F Social structure theory is the view that disadvantaged economic class position is a primary cause of crime.

11. T / F Theory construction is the process of predicting individual behavior.

12. T / F An accurate measurement of crime must be valid.

13. T / F The Enron scandal is an example of white-collar crime.

14. T / F Retribution involves the treatment of criminal offenders aimed at preventing future criminal behavior.

15. T / F The purpose of equity in the criminal law is to make criminals pay back for their crimes.

Fill in the Blank

1. Criminology is an academic discipline that uses scientific methods to study the_____, _____, _____, and _____ of criminal behavior.

2. Social philosophers in the mid-eighteenth century wanted a more _____ approach to punishment.

3. The catch phrase of the classical perspective was _____.

4. Positivist criminology is the application of _____ to the study of human behavior.

5. According to Durkheim, crime is _____ because it is virtually impossible to imagine a society without it.

6. Classical theory has evolved into modern _____.

7. Deviance is behavior that departs from the social norm but is not necessarily

_____.

8. The written code that defines crimes and their punishments is known as

_____.

9. Mala prohibitum crimes are also known as _____.

10. A _____ is a minor crime usually punished by a short jail term and/or a fine.

11. _____ courts review trial court procedures to determine whether they have complied with accepted rules and constitutional doctrines.

12. Criminology is a(n) _____ science.

13. _____ is the view that people's behavior is motivated by the pursuit of pleasure and the avoidance of pain.

14. _____ is the view that disadvantaged economic class position is a primary cause of crime.

15. _____ involves the correction and control of known criminal offenders.

Essay

1. Discuss the basic elements of classical criminology.

   - Utilitarianism

   - Rational choice

   - Free will

   - Punishment

     o Swift, certain, severe

2. Discuss the main elements of Positivism.

   - Scientific method

   - Identify necessary and sufficient conditions

   - Real and observed phenomena

   - Value free

3. Discuss Durkheim's idea that as societal structure changes, anomie results, and crime occurs.

   - Link between social factors and crime

   - Societal change causes anomie (norm and role confusions)

   - Anomie leads to confusion and rebellion crime

4. Discuss the evolution of contemporary criminology.

- Classical theory evolved to rational choice theory
- Lambrosian theory has become modern trait/biosocial theory
- Chicago school has evolved to social structure theory
- 1930s and 1940s saw the beginnings of social process theories
- Marxist economic theory has influenced critical criminology and feminism

5. Discuss the purposes of the criminal law.

- enforcing social control
- discouraging revenge
- expressing opinion and morality
- deterring criminal behavior
- punishing wrongdoing
- creating equality
- maintaining social order

ANSWER KEY FOR CHAPTER REVIEW QUESTIONS

Multiple Choice

1.	(b) an interdisciplinary	p. 2
2.	(b) biological determinism	p. 4
3.	(c) Positivism	pp. 3-4
4.	(a) anomie	p. 5
5.	(b) sociological	p. 4
6.	(a) socialization	p. 5
7.	(d) Conflict	p. 7
8.	(a) validity	p. 8
9.	(d) reliable	p. 8
10.	(a) the consensus view of crime	p. 14
11.	(c) the interactionist view of crime	p. 14
12.	(b) the conflict view of crime	p. 14
13.	(c) criminal justice	p. 2
14.	(a) the scientific method	p. 4
15.	(b) sociology	p. 3
16.	(a) felony	p. 17
17.	(c) capitalism	p. 7
18.	(d)deterrence	p. 17
19.	(b) appellate	p. 23
20.	(d) Mahatma Gandhi	p. 23
21.	(a) Branding	p. 2
22.	(c) Chicago	p. 5
23.	(d) critical criminology	p. 6
24.	(c) predicting criminal behavior	p. 8
25.	(b) ex post facto	p. 9
26.	(a) white-collar	p. 10
27.	(b) penology	p. 11
28.	(a) calculating victimization	p. 12
29.	(d) Decriminalization	p. 13
30.	(c) the Mosaic code	p. 16

True/False

1. True   p. 4
2. False   p. 6
3. True   p. 5
4. False   p. 5
5. False   p. 15
6. False   p. 16
7. True   p. 16
8. True   p. 4
9. False   p. 7
10. True   p. 8
11. True   p. 9
12. True   p. 10
13. True   p. 12
14. False p. 13
15. True   p. 17

Fill In the Blank

1. nature, extent, cause, and control   p. 3
2. rational   p. 4
3. "let the punishment fit the crime"   p. 4
4. the scientific method   p. 4
5. normal   p. 6
6. rational choice theory   p. 8
7. criminal   p. 13
8. the criminal law   p. 14
9. statutory crimes   p. 16
10. misdemeanor   p. 17
11. appellate   p. 18
12. interdisciplinary   p. 3
13. utilitarianism   p. 4
14. social structure theory   p. 8
15. penology   p. 13

Essay

1. pp. 2-3
2. pp. 3-4
3. pp. 4-5
4. pp. 6-7
5. pp. 17-18

2   The Nature and Extent of Crime

LEARNING OBJECTIVES

After mastering the content of this chapter, a student should be able to:

1. Become familiar with the various forms of crime data.
2. Discuss the problems associated with collecting valid crime data.
3. Discuss the recent trends in the crime rate.
4. Identify the factors that influence crime rates.
5. Understand the patterns in the crime rate.
6. Recognize that there are age, gender, and racial patterns in crime.
7. Discuss the association between social class and crime.
8. Describe the various positions on gun control.
9. Understand Wolfgang's pioneering research on chronic offending.
10. Understand the influence the discovery of the chronic offender has had on criminology.

KEY WORDS AND DEFINITIONS

Uniform Crime Report (UCR) - Large database, compiled by the Federal Bureau of Investigation (FBI), of crimes reported and arrests made each year throughout the United States. p. 24

Part I crimes (Index Crimes) - The eight most serious offenses included in the UCR: murder, forcible rape, assault, robbery, burglary, arson, larceny, and motor vehicle theft. p. 24

Part II crimes – All crimes, including Part I crimes. p. 24

Cleared crimes – Crimes for which a person has been arrested, charged, and turned over to the courts, or when someone is beyond police control, such as having fled the country. p. 25

National Incident-Based Reporting System (NIBRS) – Program that requires police agencies to provide a brief account of each incident and arrest for 22 crime patterns. p. 27

Sampling – Selecting a limited number of people for study as a representative of a larger group. p. 28

Population – All people who share a particular characteristic such as all college students. p. 28

National Crime Victimization Survey (NCVS) - The ongoing victimization study conducted jointly by the Justice Department and the U.S. Census Bureau that surveys victims about their experiences with law violation. p. 28

Self-report surveys - A research approach that requires subjects to reveal their own participation in delinquent or criminal acts. p. 29

Instrumental crimes - Offenses designed to improve the financial or social position of the criminal. p. 40

Expressive crimes - Offenses committed not for profit or gain but to vent rage, anger, or frustration. p. 40

Aging out (desistance) - The fact that people commit less crime as they mature. p. 44

Masculinity hypothesis - The view that women who commit crimes have biological and psychological traits similar to those of men. p. 45

Liberal feminist theory – A view that suggests the social and economic role of women in society controls their crime rate. p. 46

Racial threat view - As the size of the black population increases, the perceived threat to the white population increases, resulting in a greater amount of social control imposed against blacks. p. 47

Chronic offenders/career criminals - A small group of persistent offenders who account for a majority of all criminal offenses. p. 48

Early onset – The view that repeat offenders begin their criminal careers at a very young age. p. 49

Persistence – The idea that those who start their delinquent careers early are more likely to persist as adults. p. 50

"Three Strikes" policies – Laws that require an offender to serve a life-sentence after being convicted of a third felony. p. 50

CHAPTER SUMMARY

There are several primary sources of crime statistics. The most important is the Uniform Crime Report, based on police data accumulated by the FBI. A second is the National Incident-Based Reporting System which provides brief accounts of each incident and arrests. In addition there are the National Crime Victimization Survey, a comprehensive, nationwide survey of victimization in the United States, as well as self-reports from criminal behavior surveys; and victim surveys.

Each data source has its strengths and weaknesses, and, although quite different from one another, they actually agree on the nature of criminal behavior. The crime data indicate that rates have declined significantly in the past few years and are now far less than they were a decade ago. Suspected causes for the crime rate drop include an increasing prison population, more cops of the street, the end of the crack epidemic, the availability of abortion, and the age structure of society. The data sources show stable patterns in the crime rate. Ecological patterns show that crime varies by season (higher in the warmer months) and by urban (higher) versus rural environment.

There is also evidence of gender patterns in the crime rate: Men commit more crime than women. Age also influences crime. Young people commit more crime than the elderly. Crime data show that people commit less crime as they age, but the significance and cause of this pattern are still not completely understood. Similarly, racial and class patterns appear in the crime rate. Being unable to obtain goods and services through conventional means causes some to resort to instrumental crime, offenses designed to improve the financial or social position of the criminal. Additionally, those that live in poverty are believed to commit a disproportionate amount of expressive crimes, crime designed to vent rage, anger and frustration. However, it is still unclear whether these are true differences or a function of discriminatory law enforcement.

One of the most important findings in the crime statistics is the existence of the chronic offender, a repeat criminal responsible for a significant amount of all law violations. Chronic offenders begin their careers early in life and, rather than aging out of crime, persist into adulthood. A controversial public policy response is "three strikes" laws that require offenders convicted of a third felony to serve life in prison.

CHAPTER OUTLINE

I. The Primary Sources of Crime Data
   A. Official Records: Uniform Crime Report (UCR)
      1. Part I Crimes
         a) murder and negligent homicide
         b) forcible rape
         c) robbery
         d) aggravated assault
         e) burglary
         f) larceny
         g) arson
         h) motor vehicle theft
      2. Part II Crimes
   B. PROFILES IN CRIME: FEMA fraud
   C. Compiling the UCR
   D. Validity of the UCR
      1. Non-reporting
      2. Police Errors
      3. Methodology
   E. The National Incident-Based Reporting System (NIBRS): The Future of the Uniform Crime Report
      1. FBI
      2. 46 Specific Offenses
      3. Uniformity of Reporting
   F. Survey Research
      1. Sampling
      2. Population
   G. The National Crime Victimization Survey (NCVS)
      1. National Sample
         a) 84,000 Households
         b) 149,000 People age 12 or older

       2. Validity of the NCVS

         a) Unreported Crime

         b) Overreported Crime

         c) Methodology

   H. Self-Report Surveys

       1. Focus on Juvenile Delinquency and Youth Crime

       2. Validity of Self-Reports

         a) Monitoring for the Future Study

   I. Evaluating Crime Data

II. Crime Trends

   A. CURRENT ISSUES IN CRIME: Explaining Crime Trends

   B. Trends in Violent Crime

       1. Downward Trend Last Decade

       2. Recent Increase in Violent Crimes

   C. Trends in Property Crime

       1. Slight Decline in Recent Years

       2. 10,000,000 Reported in 2005

   D. Trends in Victimization Data (NCVS Findings)

   E. Trends in Self-Reports

       1. Trends in Drug Use

       2. Monitoring the Future survey

   F. What the Future Holds

III. Crime Patterns

   A. The Ecology of Crime

       1. Day, Season and Climate

       2. Temperature

       3. Region

   B. Use of Firearms

   C. POLICY AND PRACTICE IN CRIMINOLOGY: Should Guns Be Controlled?

   D. Social Class, Socioeconomic Conditions and Crime

       1. Instrumental v. Expressive crimes

       2. Social class and Self-reports

         a) social economic class and official processing

         b) system bias

   E. Age and Crime

       1. Younger v. older

       2. Aging Out of Crime

F. Gender and Crime
1. Men v. Women
2. Trait differences
a) Masculinity Hypothesis
3. Socialization Differences
4. Cognitive Differences
5. Social/Political Differences
a) Liberal Feminist Theory
G. Race and Crime
1. Racism and discrimination
a) Racial Threat Theory
2. Economic and Social Disparity
3. Family Dissolution
IV. Chronic Offenders/Criminal Careers
A. What Causes Chronicity?
B. Implication of the Chronic Offender Concept
1. Persistence
2. "Three-strikes"

CRITICAL THINKING QUESTIONS

1. Ask your friends if they have ever committed a crime. Then ask them to provide a brief account of the incident such as requested in the NIBRS. Was there more than one crime to the incident?

2. Find crime data on your town for the past 5 years. Does it match current national trends discussed on pages 34-35 of your text?

3. Test the idea that there is a connection between temperature and crime. Chart arrest rates in your town and cross check against temperatures for the day. Is there a correlation?

4. Do you know anyone who has used a gun in self defense? Who? What were the circumstances? Does that event influence your opinion regarding gun ownership?

CHAPTER REVIEW QUESTIONS

Multiple Choice

1. The relationship between guns and _____ may influence the crime rate.
a. the economy
b. age
c. social malaise
d. abortion

2. The UCR reports
    a. only minor offenses.
    b. only PART I crimes such as murder.
    c. only the results of criminal self-reports.
    d. only the most serious crime committed during a criminal event.

3. When police have identified an individual as the perpetrator of a crime, that crime is
    a. registered.
    b. reported
    c. cleared.
    d. measured

4. Aggravated assault is usually accompanied by
    a. entering of a household.
    b. sexual assault.
    c. auto theft.
    d. use of a weapon.

5. _____ crimes are committed to vent rage or frustration.
    a. Expressive
    b. Instrumental
    c. Terminal
    d. Regressive

6. _____ crimes are those that are committed for profit.
    a. Expressive
    b. Instrumental
    c. Terminal
    d. Regressive

7. Crime is more likely to occur in
    a. rural areas.
    b. urban areas.
    c. Amish areas.
    d. suburban.

8. Crime tends to be highest among the
    a. the lower class.
    b. the upper class.
    c. the middle class.
    d. the super wealthy.

9. Persistent offenders are referred to as
    a. closet criminals.
    b. chronic offenders.
    c. majority offenders.
    d. petty offenders.

10. Interviewing 42,000 out of millions of households is an example of a
    a. population.
    b. grouping.
    c. sample.
    d. cohort.

11. The reason why some people may not report crime to the police is because
    a. they may believe victimization is a private matter.
    b. they do not have access to police services.
    c. the victimization was not important to the criminal.
    d. they trust the police.

12. Over-reporting of criminal victimization in victim surveys results from
    a. the embarrassment of reporting the crime to the interviewer.
    b. sampling error.
    c. inadequate question format.
    d. the victims' misinterpretation of events.

13. The basic assumption of self-report studies is
    a. accurate victimization rates.
    b. the most valid official data possible.
    c. their inaccuracy.
    d. the assurance of anonymity and confidentiality.

14. Which data source remains the standard unit of analysis upon which most criminological research is based?
    a. the UCR
    b. self-report data
    c. victimization data
    d. census

15. Self-reports provide information on
    a. police response times.
    b. FBI arrests.
    c. changes in victim distribution.
    d. offender characteristics.

16. The unlawful entry of a structure to commit a felony or a theft is the crime of
    a. aggravated assault.
    b. highway robbery
    c. burglary.
    d. theft.

17. The National Crime Victimization Survey (NCVS) is conducted by
    a. the FBI and DEA.
    b. the Justice Department and U.S. Census Bureau.
    c. the State Department and State Governments.
    d. the President and Congress.

18. In 2005, there were approximately _____ property crimes.
    a. 1,000,000
    b. 5,000,000
    c. 10,000,000
    d. 50,000,000

19. The NCVS samples more than _____ annually to estimate crime victimization.
    a. 10,000 school children
    b. 50,000 elderly
    c. 84,000 households
    d. 500,000 police officers

20. Crime rates peaked in _____ before beginning to decline.
    a. the 1960s
    b. the 1970s
    c. the 1980s
    d. the 1990s

21. The UCR relies on the input of
    a. 17,000 police agencies
    b. 45,000 victim surveys
    c. 23,000 self-surveys
    d. 6,000 inmate interviews

22. _____ is defined as any willful or malicious burning or attempted burn a dwelling, motor vehicle or aircraft.
    a. Murder
    b. Arson
    c. Rape
    d. Larceny

23. _____ is the most commonly occurring crime.
    a. Murder
    b. Arson
    c. Rape
    d. Larceny

24. Only the _____ requires local police to provide a brief account of each incident and arrest.
    a. UCR
    b. NCVS
    c. NIBRS
    d. UFCJ

25. Which of the following is NOT one of the common elements of a true experiment?
    a. random selection of subjects
    b. a control group
    c. experimental conditions
    d. researcher bias

26. The recent increase in homicides occurred in all areas of the country EXCEPT
    a. rural areas.
    b. large cities.
    c. suburban counties.
    d. small towns.

27. There are roughly _____ gang members in the U.S.
    a. 250,000
    b. 500,000
    c. 750,000
    d. 1,000,000

28. Most reported crimes occur
    a. during the winter months of December and January.
    b. during the spring months of March and April.
    c. during the summer months of July and August.
    d. during the fall months October and November.

29. People _____ when they mature and reduce their criminality.
    a. age out
    b. early onset
    c. step out
    d. move on

30. What percentage of all criminals are considered to be career criminals?
    a. 1
    b. 13
    c. 21
    d. 6

True/False

1. T / F The availability of firearms may influence the crime rate, especially the proliferation of weapons in the hands of teens.

2. T / F One factor that affects crime rates is the explosive growth in teenage gangs.

3. T / F The recent decrease in property crimes has been more dramatic than the decrease in violent crime.

4. T / F "Three strikes" laws are designed for minor offenders.

5. T / F Liberal feminist theory contends that women actually commit more crime than men.

6. T / F All experts agree that crime rates will increase in the future.

7. T / F Selling narcotics is an example of an expressive crime.

8. T / F Rape and assault are examples of expressive crimes.

9. T / F Drug use is an example of an instrumental crime.

10. T / F Younger people commit crime more often than their older peers.

11. T / F Males commit more crimes than females.

12. T / F European Americans are more likely to be victims of crime than Latinos.

13. T / F Crime is more likely to occur in rural areas.

14. T / F A small group of persistent offenders accounts for a majority of all criminal offenses.

15. T / F The later in life someone begins a criminal career, the more likely they are to persist as an adult.

Fill in the Blank

1. The FBI's _____ is an annual tally of crime reported to local police departments.

2. _____ ask respondents about their own criminal activity.

3. Some experts tie increases in the violent crime rate between 1980 and 1990 to the _____.

4. _____ were enacted to incapacitate repeat felons.

5. Violent victimization rates have declined since the year _____.

6. Very high summer temperatures can cause the body to release _____ that can affect behavior.

7. The proliferation of _____ and the high rate of lethal violence they cause is the single most significant factor separating the crime problem in the United States from the rest of the developing world.

8. _____ crimes are offenses designed to improve the financial or social position of the criminal.

9. _____ crimes are offenses committed not for profit or gain but to vent rage, anger, or frustration.

10. The fact that people commit less crime as they mature is referred to as _____.

11. When a person does not age out of crime, the person is pursuing a _____.

12. The _____ attempts to explain why a few women are responsible for the handful of crimes that women commit.

13. _____ theory focuses on the amount of social control directed at Blacks.

14. _____ are about 12 percent of the population, but account for 38% of Part I violent arrests.

15. Most self-report surveys have focused on _____.

Essay

1. Discuss the factors believed to influence the crime rate.

   - Day, season, climate, region

   - Availability of guns

   - Social class, gender, race, age

2. Why does aging out occur?

   - Maturity

   - Function of life cycle, family relationships, marriage

   - Ability to forego immediate gratification

3. Discuss the concept of the chronic offender and what it means to our understanding of criminality.

   - Early onset

   - Repeat offenders

   - Inverse relationship between punishment to offending

   - Persistence

   - Three strikes

4. Compare the UCR, NIBRS, self-reports, and victimization surveys.

   - UCR and NIBRS: police reports, NCVS: national victim survey, criminals: self-reports.

   - UCR is the most referenced.

   - All have various validity issues.

   - All show similar trends in crime.

5. Discuss the relationship between race and crime.

   - Crime is intra-racial.

   - African Americans have highest victimization rate.

   - Commit disproportionate amount of crime.

   - May be related to discrimination (i.e, racial threat theory).

   - Economic and social disparity.

   - Breakdown of the family.

ANSWER KEY FOR CHAPTER REVIEW QUESTIONS

Multiple Choice

1.	(b) Age	p. 42
2.	(d) most serious offense	p. 27
3.	(c) cleared	p. 25
4.	(d) use of a weapon	p. 25
5.	(b) expressive	p. 40
6.	(d) instrumental	p. 40
7.	(b) urban areas	p. 29
8.	(a) lower class	p. 41
9.	(b) chronic offenders	p. 48
10.	(c) sample	p. 28
11.	(a) believe victimization may be a private mater	p. 29
12.	(d) the victim's misinterpretation of events	p. 29
13.	(d) the assurance of anonymity and confidentiality	p. 29
14.	(a) The UCR	p. 24
15.	(d) offender characteristics	p. 29
16.	(c) burglary	p. 25
17.	(b) Justice Department and U.S. Census	p. 30
18.	(c) 10,000,000	p. 35
19.	(c) 84,000 households	p. 28
20.	(d) the 1990s	p. 32
21.	(a) 17,000 police agencies	p. 24
22.	(b) Arson	p. 25
23.	(d) Larceny	p. 25
24.	(c) NIBRS	p. 27
25.	(d) 85 degrees	p. 39
26.	(b) large cities	p. 39
27.	(b) 750,000	p. 35
28.	(c) during the months of July an August	p. 38
29.	(d) age out	p. 44
30.	(d) 6	p. 48

True/False

1. True   p. 34
2. True   p. 35
3. False   p. 35
4. True   p. 50
5. False   p. 46
6. False   p. 37
7. False   p. 40
8. True   p. 40
9. False   p. 40
10. True   p. 43
11. True   p. 45
12. False   p. 47
13. False   p. 29
14. True   p. 48
15. False   p. 50

Fill in the Blank

1. Uniform Crime Report   p. 24
2. Self-report surveys   p. 29
3. crack epidemic   p. 35
4. "Three strike" laws   p. 50
5. 1994   p. 32
6. stress hormones   p. 39
7. handguns   p. 39
8. Instrumental   p. 40
9. Expressive   p. 40
10. aging out   p. 44
11. criminal career   p. 48
12. The masculinity hypothesis   p. 45
13. Racial threat   p. 47
14. African American males   p. 46
15. juveniles   p. 31

Essay

1. pp. 38-48
2. p. 44-45
3. pp. 48-49
4. pp. 24-31
5. pp. 46-7

3 Victims and Victimization

LEARNING OBJECTIVES

After mastering the content of this chapter, a student should be able to:

1. Understand the concept of victimization.
2. Describe the nature of victimization.
3. Discuss the problems of crime victims.
4. Understand the costs of victimization.
5. Discuss the relationship between victimization and antisocial behavior.
6. Recognize the age, gender, and racial patterns in victimization data.
7. Discuss the association between lifestyle and victimization.
8. Understand the term "victim precipitation."
9. List the routine activities associated with victimization risk.
10. Discuss the various victim assistance programs.

KEY WORDS AND DEFINITIONS

Victimology - The study of the victim's role in criminal events. p. 53

Victimologists - Criminologists who focus on the victims of crime. p. 53

Posttraumatic stress disorder - Psychological reaction to a highly stressful event; symptoms may include depression, anxiety, flashbacks, and recurring nightmares. p. 55

Cycle of violence - Victims of crime, especially childhood abuse, are more likely to commit crimes themselves. p. 66

Victim precipitation theory - The view that victims may initiate, either actively or passively, the confrontation that leads to their victimization. p. 60

Active precipitation - Aggressive or provocative behavior of victims that results in their victimization. p. 60

Passive precipitation - Personal or social characteristics of victims that make them "attractive" targets for criminals; such victims may unknowingly either threaten or encourage their attackers. p. 60

Lifestyle theories - The view that people become crime victims because of lifestyles that increase their exposure to criminal offenders.

Deviant place theory - The view that victimization is primarily a function of where people live. p. 61

Routine activities theory - The view that victimization results from the interaction of three everyday factors: the availability of suitable targets, the absence of capable guardians, and the presence of motivated offenders. p. 63

Suitable targets - Objects of crime (persons or property) that are attractive and readily available. p. 63

Capable guardians - Effective deterrents to crime, such as police or watchful neighbors. p. 63

Motivated offenders – People willing and able to commit crimes. p. 63

Victim–witness assistance programs - Government programs that help crime victims and witnesses; may include compensation, court services, and/or crisis intervention. p. 66

Compensation - Financial aid awarded to crime victims to repay them for their loss and injuries; may cover medical bills, loss of wages, loss of future earnings, and/or counseling. p. 66

Crisis intervention - Emergency counseling for crime victims. p. 67

Victim–offender reconciliation programs - Mediated face-to-face encounters between victims and their attackers, designed to produce restitution agreements and, if possible, reconciliation. p. 67

CHAPTER SUMMARY

Criminologists now consider victims and victimization a major focus of study. About 24 million U.S. citizens are victims of crime each year. Like the crime rate, the victimization rate has been in sharp decline. The social and economic costs of crime, however, remain in the billions of dollars annually, about $1,800 per citizen annually. Victims suffer long-term consequences such as experiencing fear and posttraumatic stress disorder. Research shows that victims are more likely than nonvictims to engage in antisocial behavior and thus perpetuate a cycle of violence.

Like crime, victimization has stable patterns and trends. Violent crime victims tend to be young, poor, single males living in large cities, although victims come in all ages, sizes, races, and genders. Females are more likely than males to be victimized by somebody they know. African Americans are more likely than European Americans to be victims of crime. Adolescents maintain a high risk of being physically and sexually victimized. Their victimization has been linked to a multitude of subsequent social problems. Many victimizations occur in the home, and many victims are the target of relatives and loved ones.

There are a number of theories of victimization. One view, called victim precipitation, is that victims provoke criminals; active precipitation occurs when the victim acts provocatively; passive precipitation occurs when a victim exhibits some characteristic that threatens or encourages the aggressor. Lifestyle theories suggest that victims put themselves in danger by engaging in high-risk activities, such as going out late at night, living in a high-crime area, and associating with high-risk peers. Even living a "college lifestyle of partying and taking recreational drugs can make someone victimization prone. Deviant place theory argues that victimization risk is related to neighborhood crime rates. The routine activities theory maintains that a pool of motivated offenders exists and that these offenders will take advantage of unguarded, suitable targets.

Victim service programs help victims by providing court services, economic compensation, public education, and crisis intervention. Victim impact statements allow victims to address the court before sentencing. Victim-offender reconciliation programs encourage face-to-face mediation between victims and offenders. Most states have created a Victims' Bill of Rights. These types of programs are more developed in European countries.

CHAPTER OUTLINE

I. The Victim's Role
   - A. Victimology
   - B. Victimologists

II. Victimization's Toll on Society
   - A. Economic Loss
     1. System Costs
     2. Individual Costs
   - B. Abuse by the System
   - C. Long-Term Stress
     1. Post-traumatic Stress Disorder (PTSD)
     2. Adolescent Stress
     3. Relationship Stress
   - D. Fear
   - E. Antisocial Behavior

III. The Nature of Victimization
   - A. The Social Ecology of Victimization
   - B. The Victim's Household
   - C. Victim Characteristics
     1. Gender
     2. Age
     3. Social status
     4. Race and ethnicity
     5. Marital status
     6. Repeat victimization
        a) target vulnerability
        b) target gratifiability
        c) target antagonism
   - D. The Victims and Their Criminals

IV. Theories of Victimization
   - A. Victim Precipitation Theory
     1. Active Precipitation
     2. Passive Precipitation
   - B. Lifestyle Theories
     1. High Risk Lifestyles
     2. College Lifestyles
     3. Criminal Lifestyle

    C. Deviant Place Theory

    D. PROFILES IN CRIME: Jesse Timmendequas and Megan's Law

    E. Routine Activities Theory

        1. Suitable Targets

        2. Capable Targets

        3. Motivated Offenders

        4. Routine Activities and Lifestyle

            a) proximity to criminals

            b) time of exposure to criminals

            c) target attractiveness

            d) guardianship

    F. CURRENT ISSUES IN CRIME: Crime and Everyday Life

V. Caring for the Victim

    A. Victim Service Programs

        1. Victim Compensation

        2. Victim Advocates

        3. Victim Impact statements

        4. Public Education

        5. Crisis Intervention

        6. Victim-Offender Reconciliation Programs (VORPs)

    B. Victims' Rights

    C. POLICY & PRACTICE IN CRIMINOLOGY: Victim's Rights in Europe

CRITICAL THINKING QUESTIONS

1. Have you or someone you know been a victim of crime? Calculate the "costs" of that event (see pages 3-5 of your text).

2. What do your gender, age, social status, race and marital status suggests about your likelihood of being a victim of crime? What is it about each characteristic that you think contributes to most to that likelihood?

3. Your textbook discusses the college lifestyle as making someone victimization prone. Do you agree with that perspective? Why? Why not?

4. The University of Arizona was recently identified as having a very dangerous campus. Find information about that university and identify what you might think are some of the issues that contribute to that ranking.

CHAPTER REVIEW QUESTIONS

Multiple Choice

1. The scientific study of victims is called
   a. criminology.
   b. victimology.
   c. forensics.
   d. psychology.

2. The long-term stress associated with crime victimization resulting in depression, anxiety, flashbacks, and recurring nightmares is called
   a. posttraumatic stress disorder.
   b. disassociation condition.
   c. psychosis advancement.
   d. victimization anxiety.

3. Research shows that _____ are more likely to engage in violent behavior if they were the target of physical abuse and were exposed to violent behavior among adults they know or live with, or exposed to weapons.
   a. only African American children
   b. only girls of Asian descent
   c. boys and girls of any race
   d. only children from adopted homes

4. Victimization is not random but rather a function of _____ factors.
   a. educational and genetic
   b. personal and ecological
   c. institutional and historical
   d. ecological and political

5. The more serious violent crimes, such as rape and aggravated assault, typically take place
   a. close to the noon hour.
   b. in the early morning hours.
   c. after 6 P.M.
   d. in the early afternoon.

6. Those living in the central city have significantly _____ rates of theft and violence in comparison to suburbanites.
   a. higher
   b. lower
   c. similar
   d. dissimilar

7. Which types of homes are the most vulnerable to crime?
   a. smaller
   b. African American
   c. Eastern
   d. rural

8. Which of the following would be the most important factor(s) distinguishing a victim from a non-victim.
   a. gender
   b. type of job
   c. number of people in household
   d. height

9. Victim risk diminishes *rapidly* after age
   a. 25.
   b. 35.
   c. 45.
   d. 55.

10. People over age 65 account for about _____ percent of violent victimization.
    a. 2
    b. 4
    c. 10
    d. 15

11. According to victim precipitation theory, which type of precipitation occurs when victims act provocatively, use threats or fighting words, or even attack first?
    a. active
    b. passive
    c. lifestyle
    d. routine

12. The victim's characteristics of physical weakness or psychological distress that renders them incapable of resisting or deterring crime and makes them easy targets are called _____ factors.
    a. target vulnerability
    b. target gratifiability
    c. target antagonism
    d. target hostility

13. The victim's characteristics that include having attractive possesses are called _____ factors.
    a. target vulnerability
    b. target gratifiability
    c. target antagonism
    d. target hostility

14. The victim's characteristics that arouse anger, jealousy, or destructive impulses are called _____ factors.
    a. target vulnerability
    b. target gratifiability
    c. target antagonism
    d. target hostility

15. Victims report that most crimes were committed by
    a. several criminals under the age of 18
    b. a single perpetrator, over 20.
    c. several criminals over the age of 30.
    d. a single perpetrator under the age of 16

16. According to the _____ theory, victims do not encourage crime, but are victim prone because they reside in socially disorganized high-crime areas where they have the greatest risk of coming into contact with criminal offenders, irrespective of their own behavior or lifestyle.
    a. lifestyle
    b. victim precipitation
    c. routine activities
    d. deviant place

17. Routine activities theory examines the interaction of three variables that reflect the routine activities of the typical American lifestyle. Which of the following is not one of those variables?
    a. availability of suitable targets
    b. absence of capable guardians
    c. absence of suitable targets
    d. presence of motivated offenders

18. Which of the following terms suggests a greater likelihood of victimization?
    a. college life style
    b. pre-school life style
    c. monastic life style
    d. retired life style

19. Surveys show that over _____ percent of the general public have been victimized by crime at least once in their lives.
    a. 25
    b. 50
    c. 75
    d. 90

20. An estimated _____ victim witness assistance programs have been developed throughout the United States.
    a. 2,000
    b. 20,000
    c. 200,000
    d. 350,000

21. Which of the following statements is TRUE regarding crime victims?
    a. People who are victims of crime are less likely to engage in anti-social behavior themselves.
    b. Crime victims become fearful and go through a fundamental life change.
    c. PTSD affects only adults.
    d. Children under 12 have the highest rate of victimization.

22. Two-thirds of all _____ report that they knew or were related to the offender.
    a. whites
    b. blacks
    c. men
    d. women

23. Which of the following would be the MOST likely victim of a violent assault?
    a. wealthy woman
    b. middle-class male
    c. lower-class widow
    d. homeless male

24. Which of the following statements is FALSE regarding crime victims?
    a. Males are more often victims than females.
    b. Younger, single people are more often targets than older, married people.
    c. Rates of victimization are lowest among African American males.
    d. Some people and places are targets of repeat victimization.

25. People who drinking excessively, buy and sell drugs, and engage in other criminal behavior have _____ that increase their likelihood of becoming a crime victim.
    a. high risk lifestyles
    b. deviant vocational skills
    c. low-level crime precipitation
    d. chronic activities connections

26. You have just organized a neighborhood watch; you have just increased the _____ in your community.
    a. suitable targets
    b. motivated offender
    c. capable guardians
    d. indifferent precipitators

27. Which of the following statements is TRUE?
    a. Most crimes are completely random acts.
    b. Some people live in places that are magnets for crime.
    c. Illegal drug use decreases one's likelihood being a crime victim.
    d. Victims never provoke criminals.

28. Which of the following is NOT a service provided to crime victims?
    a. Counselors who explain the criminal justice process.
    b. Advocates who provide rides to and from the courthouse.
    c. Counselors who help victims negotiate the legal and medical systems.
    d. Lay judges who help victims select the penalty for the criminal.

29. Currently, _____ states have created a Victims' Bill of Rights.
    a. all
    b. most
    c. few
    d. no

30. The total cost of the justice system, legal costs, treatment cost etc. is _____ per year.
    a. $450,000,000,000
    b. $250,000,000
    c. $23,000,000
    d. $1,800,000

True/False

1. T / F Research shows that both boys and girls are more likely to engage in violent behavior if they were the target of physical abuse or were exposed to violent behavior among adults they know or live with, or exposed to weapons.

2. T / F The long-term stress associated with crime victimization resulting in depression, anxiety, flashbacks, and recurring nightmares is called victimization anxiety.

3. T / F The more serious violent crimes, such as rape and aggravated assault, typically take place during the daytime.

4. T / F Less serious forms of violence, such as unarmed robberies and personal larcenies like purse snatching, are more likely to occur during the daytime.

5. T / F Rural, European-American homes in the Northeast are the least likely to be vulnerable to crime.

6. T / F Renters are less vulnerable to crimes than people who own their own homes.

7. T / F Females are more likely than males to be the victims of violent crime.

8. T / F Men are almost twice as likely as women to experience robbery.

9. T / F Gender differences in the victimization rate appear to be increasing.

10. T / F Females are most often victimized by someone they knew.

11. T / F Showing physical weakness is an example of target antagonism.

12. T / F Capable guardians include teenage boys.

13. T / F Suitable targets for crime include unlocked homes.

14. T / F Less than half of all victim programs include public education.

15. T / F Most victim programs refer victims to specific services to help them recover from their ordeal.

Fill in the Blank

1. Scholars who focus their attention on crime victims are called _____.

2. The TOTAL loss due to crime is estimated to be _____.

3. There is growing evidence that crime victims are _____ likely to commit crimes themselves.

4. People, especially young _____, who are physically or sexually abused, are much more likely to smoke, drink, and take drugs than are non-abused youth.

5. Individuals who have been victims of crime have a significantly _____ chance of being victims in the future.

6. Crime victimization tends to be _____ racial since both victim and perpetrator tend to be of the same race.

7. Women were _____ likely than men to be robbed by a friend or acquaintance.

8. Victims report that _____ is a factor in 33% of all incidents.

9. _____ precipitation occurs when the victim exhibits some personal characteristic that unknowingly either threatens or encourages the attacker.

10. Some people live in places that are magnets for _____.

11. Some experts link victimization to _____ lifestyles such as gang membership or drug dealing.

12. One of the primary goals of victim advocates has been to lobby for legislation creating crime victim _____ programs.

13. Emergency counseling for victims is called _____.

14. Victim-Offender Reconciliation Programs use _____ to facilitate face-to-face encounters between victims and their attackers.

15. Most jurisdictions allow victims to make a _____ before the sentencing judge.

Essay

1. Explain potential reasons for the decline in household victimization rates during the last fifteen years.

   - Population movement and changes.

   - Movement to rural areas.

   - Reduced family size.

   - More single-person homes.

2. Discuss the interaction of three variables that reflect the routine activities of the typical American lifestyle and the relationship of those variables to victimization.

   - Every society has some people willing to commit crime.

   - Volume and distribution of predatory crime is a product of the interaction of

     o Availability of suitable targets

     o Lack of capable guardians

     o Presence of motivated offenders

   - Closely related to life style approach.

3. Discuss Deviant Place Theory and the role of place in victimization risk.

    - Crime is a function of where people live.

    - Higher risk of coming into contact with criminals.

    - Poor, densely populated, highly transient neighborhoods.

4. Discuss posttraumatic stress disorder and how it can result from crime victimization.

    - Can leads to depression, anxiety and self-destructive behavior.

    - Adolescent, relationship stress.

    - Fear and ant-social behavior.

    - Cycle of violence.

5. Discuss the general rights included in most states' Victims' Bill of Rights.

    - Notification of proceedings.

    - Present at proceedings.

    - Allowed to make statements.

    - Speedy trial.

    - Confidentiality.

ANSWER KEY FOR CHAPTER REVIEW QUESTIONS

Multiple Choice

1.	(b) victimology	p. 53
2.	(a) posttraumatic stress disorder	p. 53
3.	(c) boys and girls of any race	p. 55
4.	(b) personal and ecological	p. 56
5.	(c) after 6 P.M.	p. 56
6.	(a) higher	p. 57
7.	(b) African-American	p. 57
8.	(a) gender	p. 57
9.	(a) 25	p. 58
10.	(a) 2%	p. 58
11.	(a) active	p. 60
12.	(a) target vulnerability	p. 59
13.	(b) target gratifiability	p. 59
14.	(c) target antagonism	p. 59
15.	(b) single, perpetrator over 20	p. 60
16.	(d) deviant place	p. 61
17.	(c) absence of suitable targets	p. 63
18.	(a) college life style	p. 61
19.	(c) 75	p. 65
20.	(a) 2,000	p. 66
21.	(b) crime victims becoming fearful	p. 55
22.	(d) women	p. 57
23.	(d) homeless male	p. 58
24.	(c) Rates are lowest among African American males	p. 58
25.	(a) high risk lifestyles	p. 60
26.	(c) capable guardians	p. 63
27.	(b) Some people live in places that are magnets for crime	p. 61
28.	(a) Lay judges who help select the penalty	p. 66
29.	(a) All	p. 67
30.	(a) $450,000,000	p. 54

True/False

1.	True	p. 55
2.	False	p. 55
3.	False	p. 56
4.	True	p. 57
5.	True	p. 57
6.	False	p. 57
7.	False	p. 57
8.	True	p. 57
9.	False	p. 58
10.	True	p. 57
11.	False	p. 59
12.	False	p. 63
13.	True	p. 63
14.	False	p. 67
15.	True	p. 66

Fill in the Blank

1.	victimologists	p. 53
2.	$450,000,000	p. 54
3.	more	p. 56
4.	males	p. 57
5.	higher	p. 59
6.	intra	p. 60
7.	more	p. 57
8.	substance abuse	p. 60
9.	Passive	p. 60
10.	criminals	p. 62
11.	high-risk	p. 63
12.	compensation	p. 66
13.	crisis intervention	p. 67
14.	mediators	p. 67
15.	victim impact statement	pp. 66-67

Essay

1.	p. 57
2.	pp. 63-64
3.	pp. 61-62
4.	p. 55-56
5.	p. 67

4   Choice Theory: Because They Want To

LEARNING OBJECTIVES

After mastering the content of this chapter, a student should be able to:

1. Understand the concept of rational choice.
2. Know the work of Beccaria.
3. Discuss the concepts of offense and offender-specific crime.
4. Discuss why violent and drug crimes are rational.
5. Summarize the various techniques of situational crime prevention.
6. Discuss the association between punishment and crime.
7. Understand the concepts of certainty, severity, and speed of punishment.
8. Understand what is meant by specific deterrence.
9. Discuss the issues involving the use of incapacitation.
10. Understand the concept of "just desert."
11. Understand the concept of "three strikes and you're out."

KEY WORDS AND DEFINITIONS

Rational choice - The view that crime is a function of a decision-making process in which the potential offender weighs the potential costs and benefits of an illegal act. p. 72-73

Choice theory - The school of thought holding that people choose to engage in delinquent and criminal behavior after weighing the consequences and benefits of their actions. p. 72-73

Classical criminology - The theoretical perspective suggesting that (1) people have free will to choose criminal or conventional behaviors; (2) people choose to commit crime for reasons of greed or personal need; and (3) crime can be controlled only by the fear of criminal sanctions. P. 72-73

Offense-specific - The idea that offenders react selectively to the characteristics of particular crimes. p. 73

Offender-specific - The idea that offenders evaluate their skills, motives, needs, and fears before deciding to commit crime. p. 73

Edgework - The excitement or exhilaration of successfully executing illegal activities in dangerous situations. p. 78

Seductions of crime - The situational inducements or immediate benefits that draw offenders into law violations. p. 78

Situational crime prevention - A method of crime prevention that seeks to eliminate or reduce particular crimes in narrow settings. p. 79

Defensible space - The principle that crime can be prevented to reduce the opportunity individuals have to commit crime. p. 79

Crime discouragers – People who serve as guardians of property or people. p. 79

Displacement - An effect of crime prevention efforts in which efforts to control crime in one area shift illegal activities to another. p. 81

Extinction - The phenomenon in which a crime prevention effort has an immediate impact that then dissipates as criminals adjust to new conditions. p. 81

Diffusion of benefits - An effect that occurs when efforts to prevent one crime unintentionally prevent another, or when crime control efforts in one locale reduce crime in other nontarget areas. p. 81

Discouragement - An effect that occurs when limiting access to one target reduces other types of crime as well. p. 81

Replacement – An effect that occurs when criminals try new offenses they had previously avoided. p. 81

General deterrence - A crime control policy that depends on the fear of criminal penalties, convincing the potential law violator that the pains associated with crime outweigh its benefits. p. 82

Specific deterrence - The view that criminal sanctions should be so powerful that offenders will never repeat their criminal acts. p. 85

Incarceration - Confinement in jail or prison. p. 86

Recidivism - Repetition of criminal behavior. p. 86

Incapacitation effect - The idea that keeping offenders in confinement will eliminate the risk of their committing further offenses. p. 86

Three strikes and you're out - Policy whereby people convicted of three felony offenses receive a mandatory life sentence. p. 88

CHAPTER SUMMARY

Choice theories assume that criminals carefully choose whether to commit criminal acts. People are influenced by their fear of the criminal penalties associated with being caught and convicted for law violations. The choice approach is rooted in the classical criminology of Cesare Beccaria, who argued that punishment should be certain, swift, and severe enough to deter crime. Today, choice theorists view crime as offense- and offender-specific. Offense-specific means that the characteristics of the crime control whether it occurs. For example, carefully protecting a home makes it less likely to be a target of crime. Offender-specific refers to the personal characteristics of potential criminals. People with specific skills and needs may be more likely to commit crime than others. Additionally, individuals reflect rationality by structuring the place and characteristics of their targets.

Research shows that offenders consider their targets carefully before deciding on a course of action. Thieves, violent criminals, and even drug addicts show signs of rationality. By implication, crime can be prevented or displaced by convincing potential criminals that the risks of violating the law exceed the benefits. Situational crime prevention is the application of security and protective devices that make it more difficult to commit crime, reduce criminal rewards, or induce guilt. Situational crime prevention also carries significant hidden benefits-the diffusion of crime-and costs such as the displacement of crime from one area to another.

Deterrence theory holds that if criminals are indeed rational, an inverse relationship should exist between punishment and crime. The certainty of punishment seems to deter crime. If people do not believe they will be caught, even harsh punishment may not deter crime. Some people are deemed to be more "deterrable" than others. Deterrence theory has been criticized on the grounds that it wrongfully assumes that criminals make a rational choice before committing crimes, that it ignores the intricacies of the criminal justice system, and that it does not take into account the social and psychological factors that may influence criminality. A big disappointment for deterrence theory is the fact that the death penalty does not seem to reduce murders. Specific deterrence theory holds that the crime rate can be reduced if known offenders are punished so severely that they never commit crimes again.

There is little evidence that harsh punishment actually reduces the crime rate. Most prison inmates recidivate. Incapacitation theory maintains that if deterrence does not work, the best course of action is to incarcerate known offenders for long periods so that they lack criminal opportunity. Research efforts have not proved that increasing the number of people in prison—and increasing prison sentences —will reduce crime rates.

CHAPTER OUTLINE

I. The Development of Rational Choice Theory
II. The Concepts of Rational Choice
    A. Offense- and Offender-Specific Crime
    B. Structuring Criminality
        1. Economic Need/Opportunity
        2. False Expectations
        3. Personal Traits and Experiences
        4. Learning Criminal Techniques
    C. Structuring Crime
        1. Choosing the Place
        2. Choosing Targets
III. Is Crime Rational?
    A. Is Theft Rational?
    B. PROFILES IN CRIME: Copping the Cappers
    C. Is Drug Use Rational
    D. Can Violence Be Rational?
IV. Why Do People Commit Crime?
    A. Edgework
    B. The Seduction of Crime
V. Controlling Crime

VI. Situational Crime Prevention

    A. Crime Prevention Strategies

        1. Increase the Effort Needed to Commit Crime

        2. Increase the Risk of Committing Crime

        3. Reduce the Rewards of Crime

        4. Induce Guilt

        5. Reduce Provocation

        6. Remove Excuses

    B. POLICE & PRACTICE IN CRIMINOLOGY: CCTV or Not CCTV? Comparing Situational Crime Prevention Efforts in Britain and the United States

    C. Costs and Benefits of Situational Crime Prevention

        1. Hidden Benefits

            a) diffusion

            b) discouragement

        2. Hidden Costs

            a) displacement

            b) extinction

            c) replacement

VII. General Deterrence

    A. Certainty of Punishment

    B. Police and Certainty of Punishment

    C. Severity of Punishment

    D. CURRENT ISSUES IN CRIME: Does Capital Punishment Deter Murder?

    E. Swiftness of Punishment

    F. Critique of General Deterrence

        1. Rationality

        2. Certainty, Severity, and Speed

        3. "Deterrability"

VIII. Specific Deterrence

    A. Recidivism

    B. Incarceration

IX. Incapacitation

    A. Can Incapacitation Reduce Crime?

X. Policy Implications of Choice Theory

CRITICAL THINKING QUESTIONS

1. If you or someone you know has committed a crime, utilize the elements of structuring criminality to explain the decision to engage in criminality.

2. Is there any behavior that you would conclude is completely irrational?

3. The British have utilized closed circuit television at a rate higher than the United States. How might the US better utilize this technology? Would you use it on campus? Where?

4. Page 82 of your text features a section on illegal music downloads. How effective do you think these efforts have been? Have they worked on you and your friends? What type of punishment would it take, do you suppose, to deter illegal downloads?

CHAPTER REVIEW QUESTIONS

Multiple Choice

1. Using situational crime prevention strategies, which of the following is NOT a technique designed to increase perceived risks?
   a. entry/exit screening
   b. tougher laws
   c. surveillance by employees
   d. natural surveillance

2. According to Choice Theory, people choose to engage in delinquent and criminal behavior after weighing the _____ of their actions.
   a. costs only
   b. consequences and benefits
   c. benefits only
   d. long-term consequences

3. Rational choice theorists view crime as
   a. trait-specific.
   b. legally-specific.
   c. offender-specific.
   d. victim-specific.

4. According to the rational choice view, crime is a function of a(n) _____ process in which the potential offender weighs the costs and benefits of an illegal act.
   a. decision-making
   b. irrational
   c. psychotic
   d. deterministic

5. Sociologist Jack Katz argues that there are immediate benefits to criminality, which he labels the
   a. seduction of crime.
   b. hedonistic approach.
   c. get rich quick scheme.
   d. winner takes all approach.

6. Beccaria developed the _____ school of criminology.
   a. positivist
   b. psychological
   c. sociological
   d. classical

7. Crime prevention tactics generally fall into one of four categories. Which of the following is NOT one of those categories?
   a. increase the effort needed to commit crime
   b. increase the risk of committing crime
   c. induce guilt or shame for committing crime
   d. reduce the excitement received from committing the crime.

8. Target reduction strategies are designed to
   a. induce guilt or shame for committing crime.
   b. increase the sentences for youthful offenders.
   c. reduce the value of crime to the potential criminal.
   d. allow police departments to hire more officers.

9. The concept of _____ holds that the decision of numerous members of society to commit crime can be controlled by the threat of criminal punishment.
   a. specific deterrence
   b. general deterrence
   c. specific positivism
   d. general positivism

10. According to deterrence theory, crime persists because most criminals believe
    a. there is only a small chance they will be arrested for committing a particular crime.
    b. that police officers will assault them if they are caught.
    c. that if apprehended they will go to a nice prison.
    d. they are likely to be punished quickly.

11. In the _____, criminologists focusing on classical ideas of the past, expounded the theme that criminals are rational actors.
    a. 1880s
    b. 1950s
    c. 1960s
    d. 1980s

12. Armed robbers' familiarity with the area gives them ready knowledge of escape routes and is referred to as
    a. crime space.
    b. awareness space.
    c. rational space.
    d. defensible space.

13. According to _____ Gary Becker, criminals engage in a cost-benefit analysis.
    a. politician
    b. criminologist
    c. economist
    d. psychologist

14. According to classical criminology, crime can be controlled only by
    a. religious guilt.
    b. fear of punishment.
    c. increased due process protections.
    d. correct medical treatments.

15. Research shows that robbery levels are relatively _____ in neighborhoods where residents keep a watchful eye on the neighbor's property.
    a. high
    b. low
    c. unstable
    d. unchanged

16. Violent offenders avoid victims who may be
    a. armed and dangerous.
    b. nonviolent.
    c. under the influence.
    d. drug dealers.

17. According to rational choice theorists, crime is _____ because criminals evaluate their own skills, motives, and needs.
    a. offense-specific
    b. trait-specific
    c. offender-specific
    d. ecologically-specific

18. Choice theory can be traced to Beccaria's view that crime is rational and can be prevented by punishment that is _____, severe, and certain.
    a. swift
    b. retributive
    c. harsh
    d. none of the above

19. _____ refers to the "exhilarating, momentary integration of danger, risk, and skill" that motivates an offender.
    a. Contracting
    b. Edgework
    c. Courage building
    d. Psyching

20. Research on the direct benefits of incapacitation
    a. has been inconclusive.
    b. indicates that incapacitation actually increases the chance of re-offending.
    c. indicates that incapacitation is an effective deterrent to criminal behavior.
    d. the benefits of incapacitation have not been studied.

21. According to rational choice theory, law violating behavior is the product of
    a. poor parenting.
    b. genetic engineering.
    c. careful thought and planning.
    d. capitalism.

22. Which of the following statements is TRUE regarding the structuring of criminality?
    a. Drug users commit less a crime as their drug habit increases.
    b. Criminal rewards always conform to criminal expectations.
    c. Criminals are "self-taught" and rarely learn criminal techniques from others.
    d. Criminals appear to be more impulsive and have less self control than others.

23. Which of the following seems to have the LEAST effect on shaping criminality and structuring crime?
    a. age
    b. socio-economic status
    c. opportunity
    d. race

24. Which of the following statements SUPPORTS rational choice theory?
    a. Drug users and dealers rarely attempt to conceal their behavior.
    b. Even serial killers use cunning and thought to avoid detection.
    c. People who cannot control their hormones commit most crime.
    d. Burglars prefer to rob crowded house, rather than empty ones.

25. By installing better lighting, deadbolts locks, and security cameras around your dorm, your university has created
    a. an aggressive garden.
    b. ecological persistence.
    c. crime perimeters.
    d. defensible space.

26. Publishing "John lists" is an attempt to _____ as a means of deterring the soliciting of prostitutes.
    a. reduce the reward of crime
    b. increase the effort needed to commit crime
    c. induce guilt
    d. remove excuses

27. When efforts to prevent one crime unintentionally prevent another, it is known as
    a. contrition.
    b. diffusion.
    c. extinction.
    d. reflection.

28. _____ occurs when crime control efforts simple move or redirect offenders to less guarded targets.
    a. Collapse
    b. Extinction
    c. Indication
    d. Displacement

29. _____ is a crime control policy that depends on convincing the potential law violators that the pain associated with crime outweighs its benefits.
    a. Structural Marxism
    b. Latent fear
    c. General deterrence
    d. Social Strain

30. _____ is the repetition of criminal behavior.
    a. Duplication
    b. Recidivism
    c. Counteraction
    d. Imitation

31. Research on the direct benefits of incapacitation _____.
    a. has been inconclusive
    b. indicates that incapacitation actually increases the chance of re-offending
    c. indicates that incapacitation is an effective deterrent to criminal behavior
    d. the benefits of incapacitation have not been studied

True/False

1. T / F Rational choice theory has roots in the classical school of criminology.

2. T / F The concept behind rational choice theory is to let the "punishment fit the crime."

3. T / F Rational choice theorists view crime as only offender-specific and not offense-specific.

4. T / F Signs of rationality in the choices of armed robbers are reflected when they generally choose targets near their homes.

5. T / F According to the rational choice approach, most criminals carefully choose where they will commit their crimes.

6. T / F Sociologist Jack Katz argues that there are immediate benefits to criminality which he labels the seduction of crime.

7. T / F Situational crime prevention suggests that crime prevention can be achieved by reducing the opportunities people have to commit particular crimes.

8. T / F Violent offenders show rationality when they avoid victims who may be armed and dangerous.

9. T / F Diffusion of benefits occurs when efforts to prevent one crime unintentionally prevent another.

10. T / F Drug dealers are the most desirable victims of robbers.

11. T / F If committing crime is a rational choice, it follows that crime can be controlled or eradicated by convincing potential offenders that crime is a poor choice.

12. T / F A positive relationship should exist between crime rates and the severity, certainty, and speed of legal sanctions.

13. T / F If the punishment for a crime is increased and the effectiveness and efficiency of the criminal justice system are improved, then the number of people engaging in that crime should increase.

14. T / F If people believed that their criminal transgressions would result in apprehension and punishment, then only the truly irrational would commit crime.

15. T / F The certainty of punishment seems to have a greater impact on punishment than severity.

Fill in the Blank

1. _____ helps to structure crime.

2. The excitement or exhilaration of successfully executing illegal activities in dangerous situations is referred to as _____.

3. The three strikes and you're out policy gives people convicted of three felony offenses _____.

4. The concept of criminal choice has prompted the creation of justice policies which treat all offenders equally without regard for their background or personal characteristics. This is referred to as the concept of _____.

5. The just desert model suggests that _____.

6. A method of crime prevention that seeks to eliminate or reduce particular crimes in narrow settings is referred to as _____.

7. Even serial killers use cunning and thought to avoid _____.

8. An effect of crime prevention efforts in which efforts to control crime in one area shift illegal activities to another is referred to as _____.

9. Situational prevention techniques of deflecting offenders include _____.

10. An effect that occurs when limiting access to one target reduces other types of crime as well is referred to as _____.

11. _____ refers to the control of the decision to commit crime by the threat of general punishment.

12. Programs that reduce conflict by closing bars early to reduce assaults, or posting guards outside of schools to prevent taunting are ways of _____.

13. The effectiveness of punishment relies of the elements of _____, _____, and _____.

14. The view that criminal sanctions should be so powerful that offenders will never repeat their criminal acts is known as _____.

15. The repetition of criminal behavior is referred to as _____.

Essay

1. Rational choice theorists view crime as both offense- and offender-specific. Explain why this is so.

   - Criminals reactive selectively to characteristics of specific crimes.
   - Offenders assess personal skills.

2. Discuss the situational crime prevention approach.

   - Characteristics of sites and situations can affect crime.
   - Planners can deter criminal behavior by
     o Guarding targets.
     o Controlling means to commit crime.
     o Monitoring potential criminals.

3. Situational crime prevention may produce unforeseen and unwanted consequences. Discuss what is meant by displacement, extinction, discouragement, and diffusion.

   - There are hidden costs and benefits to situational crime prevention.
     o Displacement: moves crime from one place to another.
     o Extinction: short term positive effect, but criminals change tactics.
     o Discouragement: crime control efforts in one area help surrounding area.
     o Diffusion: efforts to stop one crime unintentionally deter another.

4. The theory of specific deterrence holds that criminal sanctions should be so powerful that known criminals will never repeat their criminal acts. Critique this theory. Do you agree with the basic premise of this theory? Why or why not?

   - No clear cut evidence that punishing criminals stops future criminality.
     o Mandatory arrest laws have not been shown to work.
     o May actually increase recidivism with some first time offenders.
     o Incarceration may a have a short-term effect.
     o Incapacitation effect.

5. Discuss why classical theorists consider even drug use as rational?

   - Evidence suggests onset of drug use is rational.
   - Individuals perceive benefits of drug use outweigh risk.
   - Facilitated by perception that friends and family support use.
   - Dealers utilize rational decisions about where and to whom to sell.
     o Respond to "markets" in a business-like fashion.

ANSWER KEY FOR CHAPTER REVIEW QUESTIONS

Multiple Choice

1.	(b) tougher laws	pp. 79-80
2.	(b) consequences and benefits	p. 72
3.	(c) offense-specific	p. 73
4.	(a) decision-making	pp. 72-73
5.	(a) seduction of crime	p. 79
6.	(d) classical	pp. 72-73
7.	(d) reduce excitement of committing the crime	p. 81
8.	(c) reduce the value of crime to the potential criminal	p. 80
9.	(b) general deterrence	p. 82
10.	(a) there is only a small chance of getting caught	p. 82
11.	(c) 1960s	p. 72
12.	(b) awareness space	p. 73
13.	(c) economist	p. 74
14.	(b) fear of punishment	p. 74
15.	(b) low	p. 77
16.	(a) armed and dangerous	p. 78
17.	(c) offender specific	p. 75
18.	(a) swift	p. 76
19.	(b) Edgework	p. 78
20.	(a) has been inconclusive	p. 88
21.	(c) careful thought and planning	p. 73
22.	(d) Criminals appear to be more impulsive.	p. 74
23.	(d) race	pp. 74-75
24.	(b) Even serial killers use cunning to avoid detection.	p. 78
25.	(d) defensible space	p. 79
26.	(c) induce guilt	pp. 80-81
27.	(b) discouragement	p. 81
28.	(d) displacement	p. 81
29.	(c) specific deterrence	p. 85
30.	(b) recidivism	p. 86

True/False

1. True   p. 72
2. True   p. 83
3. False   p. 73
4. True   p. 77
5. True   p. 75
6. True   p. 79
7. True   p. 79
8. True   p. 77
9. True   p. 81
10. True   p. 77
11. True   p. 82
12. False p. 83
13. False pp. 82-83
14. True   p. 82
15. True   p. 83

Fill in the Blank

1.	offense-specific	p. 73
2.	edgework	p. 78
3.	a mandatory life term without parole	p. 88
4.	false expectations	p. 74
5.	crime discouragers	p. 79
6.	situational crime prevention	p. 80
7.	detection	p. 78
8.	displacement	p. 81
9.	bus stop placement, tavern location, street closures	p. 79
10.	discouragement	p. 81
11.	general deterrence	p. 82
12.	reducing provocation	p. 81
13.	certainty, severity, speed	p. 82-83
14.	specific deterrence	p. 85
15.	recidivism	p. 86

Essay

1. pp. 73-74
2. pp. 79-81
3. p. 81
4. pp. 85-86
5. pp. 76-77

5 Trait Theory: It's in Their Blood

LEARNING OBJECTIVES

After mastering the content of this chapter, a student should be able to:

1. Understand the concept of sociobiology.
2. Explain what is meant when biosocial theorists use the term equipotentiality.
3. Discuss the relationship between diet and crime.
4. Understand the association between hormones and crime.
5. Discuss why violent offenders may suffer from neurological problems.
6. Explain the factors that make up the ADHD syndrome.
7. Discuss the role genetics plays in violent behavior.
8. Understand the concepts of evolutionary theory.
9. Discuss the psychodynamics of criminality.
10. Understand the association between media and crime.
11. Discuss the role of personality and intelligence in antisocial behaviors.

KEY WORDS AND DEFINITIONS

Trait theory - The view that criminality is a product of abnormal biological or psychological traits. p. 93

Sociobiology - The view that human behavior is motivated by inborn biological urges to survive and preserve the species. p. 94

Equipotentiality - The view that all humans are born with equal potential to learn and achieve. p. 94

Hypoglycemia - A condition that occurs when glucose (sugar) in the blood falls below levels necessary for normal and efficient brain functioning. p. 96

Androgens - Male sex hormones. p. 97

Testosterone - The principal male hormone. p. 97

Premenstrual syndrome (PMS) - The idea that several days prior to and during menstruation, excessive amounts of female sex hormones stimulate antisocial, aggressive behavior. p. 97

Neurophysiology - The study of brain activity. p. 98

Attention deficit hyperactivity disorder (ADHD) - A developmentally inappropriate lack of attention, along with impulsivity and hyperactivity. p. 100

Conduct disorder – A pattern of repetitive behavior in which the rights of others or the social norms are violated. p. 101

Neurotransmitters - Chemical compounds that influence or activate brain functions. p. 101

Arousal theory - The view that people seek to maintain a preferred level of arousal but vary in how they process sensory input. A need for high levels of environmental stimulation may lead to aggressive, violent behavior patterns. p. 101

Monozygotic (MZ) twins - Identical twins. p. 103

Dizygotic (DZ) twins - Fraternal (nonidentical) twins. p. 103

Contagion effect – The view that people become deviant when they are influenced by others with whom they are close in contact.

Cheater theory - A theory suggesting that a subpopulation of men has evolved with genes that incline them toward extremely low parental involvement. Sexually aggressive, they use deceit for sexual conquest of as many females as possible. p. 105

Psychodynamic (psychoanalytic) - Theory originated by Freud that the human personality is controlled by unconscious mental processes developed early in childhood, involving the interaction of id, ego, and superego. p. 107

Id - The primitive part of people's mental makeup, present at birth, that represents unconscious biological drives for food, sex, and other life-sustaining necessities. The id seeks instant gratification without concern for the rights of others. p. 107

Ego - The part of the personality developed in early childhood that helps control the id and keep people's actions within the boundaries of social convention. p. 107

Superego - Incorporation within the personality of the moral standards and values of parents, community, and significant others. p. 107

Disorder - Any type of psychological problem (formerly labeled neurotic or psychotic), such as anxiety disorders, mood disorders, and conduct disorders. p. 108

Schizophrenia - A severe disorder marked by hearing nonexistent voices, seeing hallucinations, and exhibiting inappropriate responses. p. 108

Oppositional defiant disorder (ODD) – A pattern of negativistic, hostile, and defiant behavior lasting at least six months. p. 108

Bipolar disorder - An emotional disturbance in which moods alternate between periods of wild elation and deep depression. p. 108

Schizophrenia – A severe disorder marked by hearing non-existent voices, seeing hallucinations and exhibiting inappropriate responses. p. 108

Behavior theory - The view that all human behavior is learned through a process of social reinforcement (rewards and punishment). p. 109

Social learning theory - The view that people learn to be aggressive by observing others acting aggressively to achieve some goal or being rewarded for violent acts. p. 109

Behavior modeling - Process of learning behavior (notably aggression) by observing others. Aggressive models may be parents, criminals in the neighborhood, or characters on television or in movies. p. 110

Cognitive theory - Psychological perspective that focuses on mental processes: how people perceive and mentally represent the world around them and solve problems. p. 111

Information-processing theory - Theory that focuses on how people process, store, encode, retrieve, and manipulate information to make decisions and solve problems. p. 111

Personality - The reasonably stable patterns of behavior, including thoughts and emotions, that distinguish one person from another. p. 112

Antisocial personality - Combination of traits, such as hyperactivity, impulsivity, hedonism, and inability to empathize with others, that make a person prone to deviant behavior and violence; also referred to as sociopathic or psychopathic personality. p. 112

Nature theory - The view that intelligence is largely determined genetically and that low intelligence is linked to criminal behavior. p. 114

Nurture theory - The view that intelligence is not inherited but is largely a product of environment. Low IQ scores do not cause crime but may result from the same environmental factors. p. 114

Primary prevention programs - Programs, such as substance abuse clinics and mental health associations, that seek to treat personal problems before they manifest themselves as crime. p. 114

Secondary prevention programs - Programs that provide treatment such as psychological counseling to youths and adults after they have violated the law. p. 114

CHAPTER SUMMARY

Trait theory holds that criminality is a product of abnormal biological or psychological traits. The earliest positivist criminologists were biologists. Led by Cesare Lombroso, these early researchers believed that some people manifested primitive traits that made them born criminals. Today their research is debunked because of poor methodology, testing, and logic. Biological views fell out of favor in the early twentieth century. In the 1970s, spurred by the publication of Edmund O. Wilson's Sociobiology, several criminologists again turned to study of the biological basis of criminality. Trait theorists often do not view everyone as having equipotentiality. People may develop physical or mental traits at birth or soon after. Contemporary trait theorists focus on human behavior and drives correlated with antisocial behavior. For the most part, the effort has focused on the cause of violent crime.

One area of interest is biochemical factors, such as diet (lack of proper vitamins and minerals), allergies, hormonal imbalances (high levels of androgens and/or testosterone), and environmental contaminants (such as lead). The conclusion is that crime, especially violence, is a function of diet, hypoglycemia, vitamin intake, hormonal imbalance, or food allergies. The PMS and "Twinkie" defenses are innovative criminal defenses based on hormonal imbalance and poor diet. Neurophysiological factors, such as brain disorders, ADHD, EEG abnormalities, tumors, and head injuries have been linked to crime. Criminals and delinquents often suffer brain impairment, as measured by the EEG and PET scans.

Attention deficit hyperactivity disorder(ADHD) and conduct disorder are related to antisocial behavior. Although the origins of ADHD are unknown, suspected causes include neurological damage, prenatal stress and chemical allergies. Three percent of U.S. children may suffer from ADHD. Arousal theorists believe crime may be the result of the difference in how a person's brain responds to environmental stimuli and a desire to maintain an optimal level of arousal. Some biocriminologists believe that the tendency to commit violent acts is inherited. Research has been conducted with twin pairs and adopted children to determine whether genes are related to behaviors. Results do suggest some link between genetics and crime. An evolutionary branch holds that changes in the human condition that have taken millions of years to evolve, may help explain crime rate differences. As the human race evolved, traits and characteristics have become ingrained. Cheater theory holds that a subpopulation of sexually aggressive men has evolved with genes that incline them toward extremely low parental involvement.

The psychodynamic view, developed by Sigmund Freud, links aggressive behavior to personality conflicts arising from childhood. The development of the unconscious personality early in childhood influences behavior for the rest of a person's life. Criminals have weak egos and damaged personalities. According to some psychoanalysts, psychotics are aggressive, unstable people who can easily become involved in crime. Children with oppositional defiant disorder, for example, experience an ongoing pattern of uncooperative defiant and hostile behavior toward authority figures. Schizophrenia is a severe mental disorder where individuals hear nonexistent voices, hallucinate and exhibit inappropriate responses.

Behavioral and social learning theorists see criminality as a learned behavior. Children who are exposed to violence and see it rewarded may become violent as adults. People commit crime when they model their behavior after others they see being rewarded for the same acts. In modern society, aggressive acts are usually modeled after family interactions, environmental experiences and mass media. Behavior is reinforced by rewards and extinguished by punishment. Psychological traits such as personality and intelligence have been linked to criminality.

Cognitive psychology is concerned with human development and how people perceive the world. Criminality is viewed as a function of improper information processing. Individual reasoning processes influence behavior. Reasoning is influenced by the way people perceive their environment. Other researchers contend that crime may be a product of an anti-social personality. Personality traits have been linked not only to antisocial behaviors such as rape and assault, but white collar crimes as well.

The controversial issue of the relationship of IQ to criminality has been resurrected once again with the publication of research studies purporting to show that criminals have lower IQs than noncriminals. The nature v. nurture debate revolves around the argument as to whether important characteristics such as IQ are products of birth, or socialization.

Social policy responses include primary prevention programs that seek to treat personal problems before they manifest themselves as crimes. Secondary prevention programs provide treatment such as psychological counseling to youths after they have violated the law.

CHAPTER OUTLINE

I. The Development of Trait Theory

II. Contemporary Trait Theory

III. Biological Trait Theories

    A. Biochemical Conditions and Crime

        1. Diet

        2. Hypoglycemia

        3. Hormonal Influences

            a) androgen

            b) testosterone

        4. Premenstrual Syndrome (PMS)

        5. Environmental Contaminants

    B. CURRENT ISSUES IN CRIME: Diet and Crime

    C. Neurophysiological Conditions and Crime

        1. Neurophysiology

        2. Attention Deficit Hyperactivity Disorder (ADHD)

        3. Brain Chemistry

        4. Arousal Theory

    D. Genetics and Crime

        1. Parental Deviance

        2. Adoption Studies

        3. Twin Behavior

            a) monozygotic twins

            b) dizygotic twins

            c) contagion effect

    E. Evolutionary Views of Crime

        1. Evolution of Gender and Crime

        2. "Cheater" Theory

    F. Evaluation of the Biological Branch of Trait Theory

IV. Psychological Trait Theories

    A. Psychodynamic Perspective

        1. Id

        2. Ego

        3. Superego

        4. Mental Disorders and Crime

            a) mood Disorder

            b) Oppositional Defiant Disorder (ODD)

        5. Crime and Mental Illness

            a) bipolar disorder

            b) schizophrenia

      B. PROFILES IN CRIME: Andrea Yates

      C. Behavioral Perspective: Social Learning Theory

      D. Social Learning Theory

      E. Cognitive Theory

      F. Personality and Crime

          1. Psychotic Personality

          2. Anti-social Personality

      G. Intelligence and Crime

          1. Nature Theory

          2. Nurture Theory

          3. IQ and Criminality

V. Social Policy Trait Theory

      A. Primary prevention Programs

      B. Secondary prevention Programs

CRITICAL THINKING QUESTIONS

1. Do you agree with the concept of equipotentiality? How would you apply it to yourself? Are you higher or lower than the "average?" What shapes your opinion in this area?

2. Keep track of your diet for 1 week. How rich is it in nutrients commonly associated with good mental health?

3. Do you know a "cheater?" What are the circumstances that support your conclusion?

4. Use the principal sources of behavior modeling to explain your own lack of criminality

CHAPTER REVIEW QUESTIONS

Multiple Choice

1. _____ occurs when blood glucose (sugar) falls below levels necessary for normal and efficient brain functioning.
   a. Hypothermia
   b. Hypoglycemia
   c. Hyporeactivity
   d. Hyposugaracetate

2. Symptoms of hypoglycemia include all of the following EXCEPT
   a. anxiety.
   b. sleepiness.
   c. depression.
   d. confusion.

3. Hormones are linked to emotional volatility and influence _____ of the neocortex.
   a. the left hemisphere
   b. the right hemisphere
   c. both hemispheres
   d. neither hemisphere

4. Besides aggressive behavior, other androgen-related male traits include
   a. obesity.
   b. drowsiness.
   c. passivity.
   d. impulsiveness.

5. Research conducted on both human and animal subjects has found that _____ exposure to unnaturally high levels of testosterone permanently alters behavior.
   a. prenatal
   b. postnatal
   c. postneonatal
   d. neonatal

6. The study of brain activity is referred to as
   a. neuropsychology.
   b. neurosociology.
   c. neurocriminology.
   d. neurophysiology/

7. What is the name for the view that people learn to be aggressive by observing others acting aggressively to achieve some goal or being rewarded for acting violent?
   a. psychodynamic theory
   b. behavioral modification theory
   c. cheater theory
   d. social learning theory

8. A developmentally inappropriate lack of attention, along with impulsivity and hyperactivity is known as
   a. attention deficit personality disorder.
   b. attention deficit criminality disorder.
   c. attention deficit hyperactivity disorder.
   d. attention deficit medical disorder.

9. _____ is the process of learning behavior (notably aggression) by observing others. Aggressive models may be parents, criminals in the neighborhood, or characters on television or in movies.
   a. Social learning
   b. Behavior modeling
   c. Oppositional defiance
   d. Arousal theory

10. Chemical compounds that influence or activate brain functions are known as
    a. neurotransformers.
    b. neurofunctioners.
    c. neurobrain power.
    d. neurotransmitters.

11. The reasonably stable patterns of behavior, including thoughts and emotions, that distinguish one person from another is called
    a. psyche.
    b. personality.
    c. subconscious.
    d. superego.

12. According to Freud, the primitive part of people's makeup which seeks instant gratification is referred to as the
    a. Id.
    b. Ego.
    c. Superego.
    d. Transego.

13. According to Freud, the part of the personality developed in early childhood that keeps people's actions within the boundaries of social convention is referred to as the
    a. Id.
    b. Ego.
    c. Superego.
    d. Transego.

14. According to Freud, the _____ is the incorporation within the personality of the moral standards and values of parents, community, and significant others.
    a. Id
    b. Ego
    c. Superego
    d. Psychodynamic

15. The term "psychotic" has been replaced today with the term
    a. neurotic.
    b. schizophrenic.
    c. psychodynamic.
    d. disorder.

16. The most serious psychodynamic disorder is
    a. anxiety disorder.
    b. passivity complex.
    c. obsessive personality.
    d. schizophrenia.

17. Psychodynamic theorists view criminals as _____ -dominated persons who suffer from one or more disorders.
    a. Id
    b. Ego
    c. Superego
    d. Psychodynamic

18. An emotional disturbance in which moods alternate between periods of wild elation and deep depression is known as
    a. narcissistic disorder.
    b. bipolar disorder.
    c. histrionic disorder.
    d. antisocial disorder.

19. Social learning theorists view violence as something learned through a process called _____ modeling.
    a. parental
    b. peer
    c. behavior
    d. family

20. Social learning theorists suggest that all of the following factors EXCEPT _____ may contribute to violent or aggressive behavior.
    a. a heightened arousal event
    b. unexpected outcomes
    c. aggressive skills
    d. expected outcomes

21. _____ is the concept that all humans have the same ability to learn and succeed.
    a. Physicality
    b. Intelligencia
    c. Normalicity
    d. Equipotentiality

22. _____ prompted a jury to lessen a guilty verdict from 1st degree murder to manslaughter based on a biochemical condition.
    a. Twinkie defense
    b. PMS defense
    c. Devil made me do it defense
    d. XYY chromosome defense

23. Which of the following is NOT one of the nutrients associated with good mental health?
    a. polyunsaturated fatty acids
    b. vitamins A and C
    c. carcinogens
    d. minerals zinc and magnesium

24. Male sex hormones are known as
    a. androgens.
    b. endrogens.
    c. earcinogens.
    d. esturgeons.

25. MRIs, PETs and BEAMS all have made it possible to
    a. measure the deterrent effects of prison.
    b. map the most violent parts of cities.
    c. view the genetic connection between criminal parents and their children
    d. assess which parts of the brain are linked to anti-social behavior.

26. Which of the following is FALSE regarding people with ADHD?
    a. They often fail to finish projects.
    b. They are less likely to use drugs or alcohol.
    c. They have difficulty organizing tasks or work.
    d. They often can not concentrate on school work.

27. Which of the following is a diagnosis often associated with ADHD?
    a. genetic anomie
    b. conduct disorder
    c. free will syndrome
    d. chronic depression

28. All things being equal, a criminal _____ is the strongest predictor of criminal behavior.
    a. father
    b. step-father
    c. mother
    d. step-mother

29. Which of the following statements is TRUE according to trait theory?
    a. PETs measure low levels of self-control in inmates.
    b. The strongest biochemical link to crime is the consumption of sugar.
    c. Neurological impairments have been linked to crime.
    d. Neighborhood aesthetics have been linked to ADHD and cognitive disorder.

30. _____ is a pattern of negative and aggressive behavior.
    a. Psychosis
    b. ADHD
    c. Conflict pathway
    d. Oppositional defiance disorder

True/False

1. T / F Biological explanations of crime fell out of favor and were abandoned in the early 20th century.

2. T / F Biosocial research has found that abnormal levels of male sex hormones, known as androgens, do in fact produce aggressive behavior.

3. T / F The link between PMS and crime is extremely strong.

4. T / F Bipolar disorder is considered a product of evolution.

5. T / F Some criminologists contend that crime is a product of nature and nurture.

6. T / F About 33 percent of U.S. children, most often boys, are believed to suffer from ADHD.

7. T / F Brain structure, brain damage, and brain chemicals are the causes of behavior in the neurophysiological perspective.

8. T / F Genetic theory holds that violence producing traits are passed from generation to generation.

9. T / F The psychodynamic perspective believes that behavior is the result of environmental contaminants.

10. T / F Genetic theory holds that violence-producing traits are found only in males.

11. T / F According to Freud, the Id develops as a result of incorporating within the personality the moral standards and values of parents, community, and significant others.

12. T / F Cognitive theory focuses on mental processes: how people perceive and mentally represent the world around them.

13. T / F In 1977 Travis Hirschi and Michael Hindelang published a widely read article linking intelligence and crime.

14. T / F The "Twinkie defense" promoted the view that biochemical conditions influence antisocial behavior.

15. T / F According to biosocial theorists, females are biologically and naturally more aggressive than males.

Fill in the Blank

1. The two major categories of trait theory are _____ and _____.

2. Biological explanations of crime once again reemerged in the early _____.

3. _____, the most abundant androgen, has been linked to criminality.

4. Criminologist Deborah Denno investigated the behavior of more than 900 African-American youths and found that _____ was one of the most significant predictors of male delinquency and persistent adult criminality.

5. Diet, hormones, and contaminants are the causes of behavior in the _____ perspective.

6. _____ is the view that people learn to be aggressive by observing others acting aggressively to achieve some goal or being rewarded for acting violent.

7. Cohort data gathered by Donald West and David Farrington indicate that a significant number of delinquent youths have _____.

8. _____ results when people are influenced by others with whom they are in close contact.

9. _____ was the forerunner of modern learning theorists who believed that people learn from one another through imitation.

10. Aggression evolving over time and aggressive males producing more offspring are causes of behavior according to the _____ perspective.

11. Biosocial research has found that abnormal levels of androgens produce _____ behavior.

12. According to cheater theory, a subpopulation of _____ has evolved with genes that incline them toward extremely low parental involvement.

13. Because twins reared apart are so similar, the _____, if anything, makes them different.

14. Brain chemistry and hormonal differences are related to aggression and _____.

15. The id seeks _____ without concern for the rights of others.

Essay

1. Trait theories have gained prominence recently. Discuss why this is the case.
   - Edmund O. Wilson
     - Biological and genetic conditions affect how behaviors are learned and perceived.
     - Linked to existing environmental structures.
   - Equipotentiality
   - Medical, psychological and technical advances and help study biological and biosocial and neurological factors.

2. Discuss how the relationship between genetics and crime has been studied and what is known from this research.
   - Human traits associated with criminality have a genetic basis.
     - Antisocial behavior is inherited.
     - Genetic makeup of parents is passed on to children.
     - Genetic abnormalities are linked to antisocial behavior.
   - Parental deviance: research supports the idea that a criminal father is linked to criminal son.
   - Adoption studies: research supports some relationship exists between biological parents' behavior and behavior of their children, even when there is no contact.
   - Twin behavior: research finds corresponding behavior of twins

3. Critique biological explanations of crime.
   - Fail to account for geographic, social, temporal and temporal patterns of crime.
   - Questionable methodology.

4. Discuss the effects of oppositional defiant disorder.

- Ongoing patterns of uncooperative and hostile behavior.
- Symptoms include:
    - Frequent loss of temper
    - Constant arguing with adults
    - Defying adults
    - Blaming others
    - Having a low opinion of self

5. Discuss the three principal sources upon which aggressive acts are usually modeled according to social learning theorists.

- Family interactions
- Environmental experiences
- Mass media

ANSWER KEY FOR CHAPTER REVIEW QUESTIONS

Multiple Choice

1.	(b) hypoglycemia	p. 96
2.	(b) dominance	p. 96
3.	(a) the left hemisphere	p. 97
4.	(d) impulsivity	p. 97
5.	(a) prenatal	p. 97
6.	(d) neurophysiology	p. 98
7.	(d) social learning theory	p. 109
8.	(c) Attention Deficit Hyperactivity Disorder	p. 100
9.	(b) behavior modeling	p. 110
10.	(d) Neurotransmitters	p. 101
11.	(b) personality	p. 112
12.	(a) Id	p. 107
13.	(b) Ego	p. 107
14.	(c) Superego	p. 107
15.	(d) disorder	p. 108
16.	(d) schizophrenia	p. 108
17.	(a) Id	p. 108
18.	(b) bipolar disorder	p. 108
19.	(c) behavior	p. 110
20.	(b) unexpected outcomes	p. 110
21.	(d) Equipotentiality	p. 94
22.	(a) Twinkie defense	p. 95
23.	(c) carcinogens	p. 96
24.	(a) androgens	p. 97
25.	(d) assess the part of brain linked to anti-social behavior	pp. 99-101
26.	(b) They are less likely to use drugs.	p. 100
27.	(b) conduct disorder	p. 101
28.	(a) father	p. 102
29.	(c) Neurological impairments have been linked to crime.	p. 99
30.	(d) Oppositional defiant disorder	p. 108

True/False

1. True   p. 93
2. True   p. 97
3. False   p. 97
4. False   p. 108
5. True   p. 114
6. False   p. 100
7. True   pp. 98-99
8. True   p. 105
9. False   p. 107
10. False   p. 111
11. False   p. 112
12. True   p. 111
13. True   p. 111
14. True   p. 95
15. False   p. 104

Fill in the Blank

1. biological and psychological   p. 94
2. 1970s   p. 94
3. Testosterone   p. 97
4. lead poisoning   p. pp. 97-98
5. biochemical   p. 95
6. Social learning theory   p. 109
7. criminal fathers   p. 102
8. cheater theory   pp. 109-110
9. Contagion effect   p. 103
10. evolutionary   p. 103-104
11. aggressive   p. 100
12. men   p. 105
13. environmental   p. 102-103
14. violence   pp. 96-97
15. instant gratification   p. 107

Essay

1. pp. 93-99
2. pp. 102-103
3. pp. 105-106
4. p. 108
5. pp. 109-110

6 Social Structure Theory: Because They're Poor

LEARNING OBJECTIVES

After mastering the content of this chapter, a student should be able to:

1. Understand the concept of social structure.
2. Explain the socioeconomic structure of American society.
3. Discuss the concept of social disorganization.
4. Explain the works of Shaw and McKay.
5. Describe what is meant by concentric zone theory.
6. Discuss the various elements of ecological theory.
7. Discuss the association between collective efficacy and crime.
8. Understand the concept of strain.
9. Explain what is meant by the term anomie.
10. Understand the concept of cultural deviance.

KEY WORDS AND DEFINITIONS

Stratified society - People grouped according to economic or social class; characterized by the unequal distribution of wealth, power, and prestige. p. 120

Social class - Segment of the population whose members are at a relatively similar economic level and who share attitudes, values, norms, and an identifiable lifestyle. p. 120

Truly disadvantaged - The lowest level of the underclass; urban, inner-city, socially isolated people who occupy the bottom rung of the social ladder and are the victims of discrimination. p. 120

Culture of poverty - A separate lower-class culture, characterized by apathy, cynicism, helplessness, and mistrust of social institutions such as schools, government agencies, and the police that is passed from one generation to the next. p. 120

Underclass - The lowest social stratum in any country, whose members lack the education and skills needed to function successfully in modern society. p. 121

Social structure theory - The view that disadvantaged economic class position is a primary cause of crime. p. 124

Social disorganization theory - Branch of social structure theory that focuses on the breakdown of institutions such as the family, school, and employment in inner-city neighborhoods. p. 125

Strain theory - Branch of social structure theory that sees crime as a function of the conflict between people's goals and the means available to obtain them. p. 125

Cultural deviance theory - Branch of social structure theory that sees strain and social disorganization together resulting in a unique lower-class culture that conflicts with conventional social norms. p. 125

Subculture - A set of values, beliefs, and traditions unique to a particular social class or group within a larger society. p. 125

Cultural transmission - Process whereby values, beliefs, and traditions are handed down from one generation to the next. p. 125

Transitional neighborhood - An area undergoing a shift in population and structure, usually from middle-class residential to lower-class mixed use. p. 127

Concentration effect - As working- and middle-class families flee inner-city poverty areas, the most disadvantaged population is consolidated in urban ghettos. p. 130

Collective efficacy - Social control exerted by cohesive communities, based on mutual trust, including intervention in the supervision of children and maintenance of public order. p. 130

Anomie - A lack of norms or clear social standards. Because of rapidly shifting moral values, the individual has few guides to what is socially acceptable. p. 133

Anomie theory - View that anomie results when socially defined goals (such as wealth and power) are universally mandated but access to legitimate means (such as education and job opportunities) is stratified by class and status. p. 133

Institutional anomie theory - The view that anomie pervades U.S. culture because the drive for material wealth dominates and undermines social and community values. p. 135

American Dream - The goal of accumulating material goods and wealth through individual competition; the process of being socialized to pursue material success and to believe it is achievable. p. 135

Relative deprivation - Envy, mistrust, and aggression resulting from perceptions of economic and social inequality. p. 135

General strain theory (GST) - The view that multiple sources of strain interact with an individual's emotional traits and responses to produce criminality. p. 136

Negative affective states - Anger, frustration, and adverse emotions produced by a variety of sources of strain. p. 136

Focal concerns - Values, such as toughness and street smarts, that have evolved specifically to fit conditions in lower-class environments. p. 139

Delinquent subculture - A value system adopted by lower-class youths that is directly opposed to that of the larger society. p. 139

Status frustration - A form of culture conflict experienced by lower-class youths because social conditions prevent them from achieving success as defined by the larger society. p. 139

Middle-class measuring rods - The standards by which authority figures, such as teachers and employers, evaluate lower-class youngsters and often prejudge them negatively. p. 141

Reaction formation - Irrational hostility evidenced by young delinquents, who adopt norms directly opposed to middle-class goals and standards that seem impossible to achieve. p. 142

Differential opportunity - The view that lower-class youths, whose legitimate opportunities are limited, join gangs and pursue criminal careers as alternative means to achieve universal success goals. p. 142

CHAPTER SUMMARY

Sociology has been the main orientation of criminologists because people in the United States live in a stratified society, one of social classes. Criminologists know that crime rates vary among elements of the social structure, that society goes through changes that affect crime, and that social interaction relates to criminality. Lower class areas produce cultures of poverty and an underclass cut off from the rest of society. Social structure theories suggest that people's place in the socioeconomic structure influences their chances of becoming criminals. Poor people are more likely to commit crimes because they are unable to achieve monetary or social success in any other way. Social structure theory includes three schools of thought: social disorganization, strain, and cultural deviance theories.

Social disorganization theory suggests that the urban poor violate the law because they live in areas in which social control has broken down. The origin of social disorganization theory can be traced to the work of Clifford R. Shaw and Henry D. McKay. After studying crime rates in and around Chicago, Shaw and McKay concluded that disorganized areas, marked by divergent values and transitional populations, produce criminality. Modern social ecology theory looks at such issues as community fear, unemployment, and deterioration. Strain theories view crime as resulting from the anger people experience over their inability to achieve legitimate social and economic success.

Strain theories hold that most people share common values and beliefs, but the ability to achieve them is differentiated by the social structure. The best-known strain theory is Robert Merton's theory of anomie, which describes what happens when people have inadequate means to satisfy their goals. Several types of adaptation strategies result in criminal behavior. Steven Messner and Richard Rosenfeld show that the core values of American culture, particularly and emphasis on wealth accumulation, produces strain. Robert Agnew suggests that strain has multiple sources and is linked to anger and frustration that people endure when their goals and aspirations are frustrated or when they lose something they value.

Cultural deviance theory combines elements of both strain and social disorganization theories. It holds that a unique value system develops in lower-class areas. Lower-class values approve of behaviors such as being tough, never showing fear, and defying authority. People perceiving strain will bond together in their own groups or subcultures for support and recognition. Subcultures are handed down from one generation to another through a process called cultural transmission. Albert Cohen links the formation of subcultures to the failure of lower-class citizens to achieve recognition from middle-class decision makers, such as teachers, employers, and police officers. Richard Cloward and Lloyd Ohlin have argued that crime results from lower-class people's perception that their opportunity for success is limited(differential opportunity). Consequently, youths in low-income areas may join criminal, conflict, or retreatist gangs.

CHAPTER OUTLINE

I. Economic Structure and Crime
   A. Problems of the Lower Class
      1. Culture of Poverty
      2. Underclass
   B. Child Poverty
   C. Minority Group Poverty
   D. RACE, CULTURE, GENDER AND CRIMINOLOGY: Bridging the Racial Divide
   E. Poverty and Crime
      1. Social Structure Theory and Crime
      2. Media Influences

II. Social Structure Theories
      1. Social disorganization theory
      2. Strain theory
         a) strain
      3. Cultural deviance theory
         a) subcultures
         b) cultural transmission

III. Social Disorganization Theory
   A. The Work of Shaw and McKay
      1. Concentric zones
      2. The legacy of Shaw and McKay
   B. The Social Ecology School
      1. Community Disorder
      2. Community Fear
      3. Community Change
      4. Poverty Concentration
      5. Collective Efficacy
         a) Informal social control
         b) Institutional social control
         c) Public social control

IV. Strain Theories
   A. Theory of Anomie
      1. Social Adaptations
         a) Conformity
         b) Innovation
         c) Ritualism
         d) Retreatism
         e) Rebellion
      2. Evaluation of Anomie Theory

B. Institutional Anomie Theory

C. Relative Deprivation Theory

D. General Strain Theory (GST)

    1. Multiple Sources of Strain

        a) Negative effective states

            (1) Failure to achieve positively valued goals

            (2) Disjunction of expectations and achievements

            (3) Removal of positively valued stimuli

            (4) Presentation of negative stimuli

    2. Consequences of Strain

    3. Coping with Strain

    4. Evaluating GST

V. Cultural Deviance Theory

A. Theory of Delinquent Subcultures

    1. Middle-class Measuring Rods

    2. Formation of Deviant Subcultures

        a) reaction formation

B. RACE, CULTURE, GENDER & CRIME

C. Theory of Differential Opportunity

    1. Gangs

        a) criminal gangs

        b) conflict gangs

        c) retreatist gangs

    2. Cultural Deviance and Social Disorganization

VI. Social Structure Theory and Public Policy

CRITICAL THINKING QUESTIONS

1. Do you and/or your parent live in a cohesive community with high levels of social control and social integration? How did you or parents contribute (or not) to the social efficacy of the neighborhood?

2. Could strain theory be applied to student misconduct such as cheating and plagiarism? How?

3. Not everyone who suffers strain resorts to crime. What coping measures have/do you employ to keep from engaging in criminal behavior.

4. Are there any focal concerns you value even though you are not likely a member of the lower class? Why?

CHAPTER REVIEW QUESTIONS

Multiple Choice

1. Segment of the population whose members are at a relatively similar economic level and who share attitudes, values, norms, and an identifiable lifestyle:
   a. stratified society
   b. social class
   c. lower class
   d. upper class

2. The lowest level of the underclass is also referred to as the _____.
   a. lower class
   b. lower lower class
   c. truly disadvantaged
   d. ultimate lower class

3. The lowest social stratum in any country, whose members lack the education and skills needed to function successfully in modern society, is referred to as the _____.
   a. culture of poverty
   b. middle class
   c. truly disadvantaged
   d. negative class

4. Social disorganization theory is the branch of social structure theory that focuses on the breakdown of institutions such as the _____ in inner city neighborhoods.
   a. family and school
   b. liquor stores and mini-marts
   c. banks and government agencies
   d. homeless shelters and career centers

5. According to strain theory, people feel _____ because they are unable to achieve success through conventional means.
   a. anger, frustration and resentment
   b. fear, anxiety and glee
   c. pressure, resentment and institutionalism
   d. hope, shame and aggression

6. The branches of social structure theory include all EXCEPT
   a. social disorganization theory.
   b. cultural deviance theory.
   c. strain theory.
   d. cheater theory.

7. Community deterioration includes all of the following EXCEPT
   a. disorder.
   b. poverty.
   c. alienation.
   d. high real estate rates.

8. The forms of collective efficacy include all of the following EXCEPT
   a. informal social control.
   b. personal social control.
   c. institutional social control.
   d. public social control.

9. Sources of institutional social control include all of the following EXCEPT
   a. families.
   b. businesses.
   c. stores.
   d. schools.

10. One of the primary sources of public social control is
    a. schools.
    b. policing.
    c. families.
    d. peers.

11. According to strain theory, the ability to achieve personal goals is stratified by
    a. age
    b. gender
    c. socioeconomic class
    d. weight

12. Merton argues that in the United States legitimate means to acquire wealth are stratified across _____ lines.
    a. class
    b. gender
    c. marital status
    d. age

13. Merton's social adaptation that occurs when individuals embrace conventional goals and also have the means to attain them is referred to as
    a. conformity.
    b. innovation.
    c. ritualism.
    d. retreatism.

14. Merton's social adaptation that involves substituting an alternative set of goals and means for conventional ones is referred to as
    a. conformity.
    b. innovation.
    c. ritualism.
    d. rebellion.

15. Merton's social adaptation that occurs when individuals accept the goals of society but are unable to attain them through legitimate means so they innovate is referred to as _____.
    a. conformity
    b. innovation
    c. retreatism
    d. rebellion

16. According to Merton, _____ occurs when people reject both the goals and the means of society and escape their lack of success.
    a. conformity
    b. innovation
    c. ritualism
    d. retreatism

17. According to Merton, _____ occurs when people gain pleasure from practicing traditional ceremonies, regardless of whether they have a real purpose or goal.
    a. innovation
    b. ritualism
    c. retreatism
    d. rebellion

18. According to Messner and Rosenfeld, the relatively high crime rates can be explained by the interrelationship of
    a. culture and anomie.
    b. anomie and institutions.
    c. culture and institutions.
    d. traits and anomie.

19. Sociologist Robert Agnew's general strain theory (GST) helps identify the _____-level influences of strain.
    a. micro and individual
    b. individual and genetic
    c. macro and societal
    d. institutional and personality

20. Agnew (GST) suggests that criminality is the direct result of the anger, frustration, and adverse emotions that emerge in the wake of destructive social relationships. He refers to these emotions as
    a. relative deprivation.
    b. general strain.
    c. negative affective states.
    d. social altruisms..

21. _____ results from society's emphasis on material wealth, and the reduction in importance of social institutions.
    a. Marxist utopia
    b. Social integration
    c. Stratified strain
    d. Institutional anomie

22. Social disorganization theory suggests that the urban poor violate the law because
    a. they suffer biological urges in excess of suburban populations.
    b. they are greatly influenced by violent television and music.
    c. they live in an area where social order has broken down.
    d. they are suffer institutional anomie.

23. Which of the following is a sign of a neighborhood in decline?
    a. a large population of elderly citizens
    b. a high rate of broken-homes
    c. a recent increase in the employment rate
    d. a lack of stores selling alcohol

24. Which of the following is NOT one of the major schools of thought in social structure?
    a. strain
    b. social disorganization
    c. cultural deviance
    d. differential association

25. _____ develop sets of values, beliefs and traditions unique to their social class or group within society.
    a. Concentrations
    b. Subcultures
    c. Strains
    d. Neighborhoods

26. You are a volunteer firefighter, and a member of the PTA. You are practicing
    a. collective efficacy.
    b. social anomie.
    c. the American dream.
    d. focal concerns.

27. Which of the following is NOT a focal concern?
    a. toughness
    b. street smarts
    c. autonomy
    d. work ethic

28. In order to buy a new car that will equal his neighbor's, your professor robs a liquor store. His crime could be explained as a product of
    a. focal concerns.
    b. cultural deviance.
    c. institutional anomie.
    d. American achievement.

29. Which of the following groups is MOST likely to suffer social disorganization?
    a. European Americans
    b. African Americans
    c. Asian Americans
    d. Elderly Americans

30. Which of the following is a public policy response based on social structure?
    a. War on Drugs
    b. War on Poverty
    c. War on Rights
    d. War on Traits

True/False

1. T / F Cultural deviance theory is a branch of social structure theory that sees strain and social disorganization together resulting in a unique lower-class culture that conflicts with conventional social norms. high crime rates.

2. T / F Cultural deviance theory argues that crime is the result of middle-class strain.

3. T / F Social disorganization theory was popularized by the work of Lombroso and Goring.

4. T / F Reaction formation is an irrational hostility evidenced by young delinquents, who adopt norms directly opposed to middle-class goals and standards that seem impossible to achieve.

5. T / F As working- and middle-class families flee inner-city poverty areas, the most disadvantaged population is consolidated in urban ghettos. This effect is known as the concentration effect.

6. T / F All one form of collective efficacy, institutional social control, contributes to community stability.

7. T / F The level of policing from neighborhood to neighborhood is typically consistent.

8. T / F Shaw and McKay found stable patterns of crime in the central city.

9. T / F Lower class measuring rods are the standards by which authority figures such as teachers evaluate upper-class youngsters.

10. T / F Agnew (GST) offers a more general explanation of criminal activity among all elements of society rather than restricting his views to lower-class crime.

11. T / F Agnew's general theory of strain suggests that there is only one source of anomie.

12. T / F Miller's lower class focus concerns include trouble, toughness, and fate.

13. T / F According to Miller, clinging to lower-class focal concerns promotes illegal or violent behavior.

14. T / F The American Dream is the goal of accumulating material goods and wealth through individual competition; the process of being socialized to pursue material success and to believe it is achievable.

15. T/F Relative deprivation suggests that envy, mistrust and aggression result from high social status and economic achievement.

Fill in the Blank

1. People in the United States live in a _____ society.

2. In 1970, Gunnar Myrdal described a worldwide _____ that was cut off from society, its members lacking the education and skills needed to function successfully in modern society.

3. Strain theory sees crime as a function of the _____ between people's _____ and the _____ available to obtain them.

4. Because crime rates are higher in lower-class areas, many criminologists believe that the causes of crime are rooted in _____ factors.

5. A set of values, beliefs, and traditions unique to a particular social class or group within a larger society is known as _____.

6. In larger cities, abandoned buildings serve as a "_____."

7. Communities characterized by mutual trust, a willingness to intervene in the supervision of children and the maintenance of public order have developed _____.

8. Schools and churches hare sources of _____ that can help reduce crime rates.

9. A lack of norms or clear social standards is referred to as _____.

10. The process of being socialized to pursue material success and to believe it is achievable is known as the _____.

11. Envy, mistrust, and aggression resulting from perceptions of economic and social inequality are referred to as _____.

12. According to Miller, the values, such as toughness and street smarts, that have evolved specifically to fit conditions in lower-class environments is referred to as _____.

13. A value system adopted by lower-class youths that is directly opposed to that of the larger society is referred to as _____.

14. The standards by which authority figures, such as teachers and employers, evaluate lower-class youngsters and often prejudge them negatively is referred to as _____.

15. Because of differential opportunity, young people are likely to join one of three types of gangs which include _____, _____, and _____.

Essay

1. Discuss the legacy of Shaw and McKay.

    *   Remains prominent after 75 years.

    *   Still applicable after important social and cultural changes.

    *   Paved the way for many community action and community programs.

2. Discuss the major sections of the social ecology school.

- Community disorder
- Community fear
- Siege mentality
- Community change
- Poverty concentration
- Collective efficacy: informal, institutional, and public controls

3. Discuss the three forms of collective efficacy and how they contribute to community stability.

- Informal social controls
  - Most important is family.
- Institutional social controls
  - Schools and churches
- Public social controls
  - Level of policing

4. Discuss Merton's social adaptations and how they relate to criminal behavior.

- Each person has his own concept of societies goals and means to attain them.
- Some have inadequate means and/or reject societies goals. Adaptations include:
  - Conformity
  - Innovation
  - Ritualism
  - Retreatism
  - Rebellion

5. What are the gang types that develop according to differential opportunity theory?

- Criminal gangs
- Conflict gangs
- Retreatist gangs

ANSWER KEY FOR CHAPTER REVIEW QUESTIONS

Multiple Choice

1.	(b) social class	p. 120
2.	(c) truly disadvantaged	p. 120
3.	(d) underclass	p. 121
4.	(d) family and school	p. 125-126
5.	(a) anger, frustration and resentment	p. 125
6.	(d) cheater theory	pp. 125-126
7.	(d) high real estate rates	p. 130
8.	(b) personal social control	p. 130
9.	(a) families	p. 130
10.	(b) policing	p. 130
11.	(c) socioeconomic class	p. 125
12.	(a) class	p. 139
13.	(a) conformity	pp. 134
14.	(d) rebellion	pp. 134
15.	(b) innovation	pp. 134
16.	(d) retreatism	pp. 134
17.	(b) ritualism	pp. 134
18.	(c) culture and institutions	pp. 136-137
19.	(a) micro and individual	p. 136
20.	(c) negative affective states	p. 136
21.	(d) Institutional anomie	p. 135
22.	(c) they live where order has broken down	p. 125
23.	(b) a high rate of broken homes	p. 126
24.	(d) differential association	pp. 120-125
25.	(b) Subcultures	p. 125
26.	(a) collective efficacy	pp. 131-132
27.	(d) work ethic	p. 139
28.	(c) institutional anomie	p. 135
29.	(b) African Americans	p. 136
30.	(c) War on Poverty	p. 144

True/False

1. True   p. 139
2. False   p. 125
3. False   p. 130
4. True   p. 127
5. True   p. 130
6. False   p. 130
7. True   p. 130
8. False   p. 130
9. False   p. 141
10. True   p. 135
11. False p. 135
12. True   p. 139
13. True   p. 139
14. True   p. 135
15. False p. 135

Fill in the Blank

1. stratified   p. 120
2. underclass   p. 121
3. conflict, goals, means   p. 125
4. socioeconomic   pp. 120-123
5. subculture   p. 125
6. magnet for crime   p. 129
7. collective efficacy   p. 130
8. institutional social control   p. 131
9. anomie   p. 133
10. American Dream   p. 135
11. relative deprivation   p. 135
12. focal concerns   p. 139
13. delinquent subculture   p. 139
14. middle-class measuring rod   p. 141
15. criminal, conflict, retreatist   pp. 142-143

Essay

1. pp. 127-9
2. pp. 128-132
3. pp. 131-132
4. pp. 134
5. pp. 142-143

7 Social Process Theories: Socialized to Crime

LEARNING OBJECTIVES

After mastering the content of this chapter, a student should be able to:

1. Explain the concept of socialization.
2. Discuss the effect of schools, family, and friends on crime.
3. Discuss the differences between learning, control, and reaction.
4. Understand the concept of differential association.
5. Discuss what is meant by a definition toward criminality.
6. Understand the concept of neutralization.
7. Discuss the relationship between self-concept and crime.
8. Explain the elements of the social bond.
9. Describe the labeling process.
10. Understand the concepts of primary and secondary deviance.
11. Explain how the process of labeling leads to criminal careers.

KEY WORDS AND DEFINITIONS

Socialization - Process of human development and enculturation. Socialization is influenced by key social processes and institutions. p. 147

Social process theory - The view that criminality is a function of people's interactions with various organizations, institutions, and processes in society. p. 147

Parental efficacy - Parents who are supportive and effectively control their children in a noncoercive fashion. p. 148

Social learning theory - The view that people learn to be aggressive by observing others acting aggressively to achieve some goal or being rewarded for violent acts. p. 150

Social control theory - The view that people commit crime when the forces binding them to society are weakened or broken. p. 150

Social reaction (labeling) theory - The view that people become criminals when labeled as such and when they accept the label as a personal identity. p. 150

Differential association theory - The view that people commit crime when their social learning leads them to perceive more definitions favoring crime than favoring conventional behavior. p. 150

Culture conflict - Result of exposure to opposing norms, attitudes, and definitions of right and wrong, moral and immoral. p. 150

Neutralization theory - The view that law violators learn to neutralize conventional values and attitudes, enabling them to drift back and forth between criminal and conventional behavior. p. 154

Drift - Movement in and out of delinquency, shifting between conventional and deviant values. P. 154

Neutralization techniques - Methods of rationalizing deviant behavior, such as denying responsibility or blaming the victim. p. 154

Self-control - A strong moral sense that renders a person incapable of hurting others or violating social norms. p. 157

Commitment to conformity - A strong personal investment in conventional institutions, individuals, and processes that prevents people from engaging in behavior that might jeopardize their reputation and achievements. p. 157

Social bonds - The ties that bind people to society, including relationships with friends, family, neighbors, teachers, and employers. Elements of the social bond include commitment, attachment, involvement, and belief. p. 158

Stigmatize - To apply negative labeling with enduring effects on a person's self-image and social interactions. p. 162

Moral entrepreneur - A person who creates moral rules that reflect the values of those in power rather than any objective, universal standards of right and wrong. p. 162

Successful degradation ceremony - A course of action or ritual in which someone's identity is publicly redefined and destroyed and they are thereafter viewed as socially unacceptable. p. 163

Retrospective reading - The reassessment of a person's past to fit a current generalized label. p. 163

Primary deviance - A norm violation or crime with little or no long-term influence on the violator. p. 164

Secondary deviance - A norm violation or crime that comes to the attention of significant others or social control agents, who apply a negative label with long-term consequences for the violator's self-identity and social interactions. p. 164

Deviance amplification - Process whereby secondary deviance pushes offenders out of mainstream of society and locks them into an escalating cycle of deviance, apprehension, labeling, and criminal self-identity. p. 164

Reflected appraisal - When parents are alienated from their children, their negative labeling reduces their children's self-image and increases delinquency. p. 166

Diversion programs - Programs of rehabilitation that remove offenders from the normal channels of the criminal justice process, thus avoiding the stigma of a criminal label. p. 169

Restitution - Permitting an offender to repay the victim or do useful work in the community rather than face the stigma of a formal trial and a court-ordered sentence. p. 169

CHAPTER SUMMARY

Social process theories view criminality as a function of people's interaction with various organizations, institutions, and processes in society. People in all walks of life have the potential to become criminals if they maintain destructive social relationships. Improper socialization is a key component of crime. Social process theory has three main branches. Social learning theory stresses that people learn how to commit crimes. Social control theory analyzes the failure of society to control criminal tendencies. Labeling theory maintains that negative labels produce criminal careers.

Social learning theory suggests that people learn criminal behaviors much as they learn conventional behavior. Differential association theory, formulated by Edwin Sutherland, holds that criminality is a result of a person's perceiving an excess of definitions in favor of crime over definitions that uphold conventional values. Sykes and Matza's theory of neutralization stresses that youths learn behavior rationalizations that enable them to overcome societal values and norms and break the law.

Control theory maintains that all people have the potential to become criminals, but their bonds to conventional society prevent them from violating the law. This view suggests that a person's self-concept aids his or her commitment to conventional action. Travis Hirschi's social control theory describes the social bond as containing elements of attachment, commitment, involvement, and belief. Weakened bonds allow youths to behave antisocially.

Social reaction or labeling theory holds that criminality is promoted by becoming negatively labeled by significant others. Such labels as "criminal," "ex-con," and "junkie" isolate people from society and lock them into lives of crime. Labels create expectations that the labeled person will act in a certain way; labeled people are always watched and suspected. Eventually these people begin to accept their labels as personal identities, locking them further into lives of crime and deviance. Edwin Lemert suggests that people who accept labels are involved in secondary deviance while primary deviants are able to maintain an undamaged identity. Unfortunately, research on labeling has not supported its major premises. Critics have charged that it lacks credibility as a description of crime causation.

CHAPTER OUTLINE

I. Socialization and Crime

    A. Family Relations

    B. Educational Experience

    C. Peer Relations

    D. Religious Belief

    E. The Effects of Socialization on Crime

II. Social Learning Theories

    A. Differential Association Theory

    B. Neutralization Theory

    C. CURRENT ISSUES IN CRIME: When Being Good is Bad

    D. Are Learning Theories Valid?

CRITICAL THINKING QUESTIONS

1. Review the important elements of social process that contribute to a criminal or non-criminal career. How do those major areas apply to you?

2. Social learning contends that even criminal techniques must be learned. Do you know any? How did you learn them?

3. View the scale on page 153 of your text. Have you been exposed to ideas on either side of the scale? From whom and under what circumstances?

4. Are you a fan of *The Simpsons*? Apply social bond to explain Bart Simpson's often antisocial behavior.

CHAPTER REVIEW QUESTIONS

Multiple Choice

1. Parents who are supportive and effectively control their children in a noncoercive fashion are more likely to raise children who refrain from delinquency. This is referred to as _____.
   a. socialization
   b. social efficacy
   c. parental efficacy
   d. social process

2. The theory that criminality is a function of people's interactions with various organizations, institutions, and processes in society is known as _____ theory.
   a. social learning
   b. social process
   c. social control
   d. social reaction

3. Children who _____ are the most likely to engage in criminal acts.
   a. do poorly in school
   b. have educational motivation
   c. feel empathy towards their neighbors
   d. have a strong relationship with their parents

4. Schools label students when they use the _____ system which identifies some students as college-bound and others as academic underachievers or potential dropouts.
   a. IQ
   b. reading
   c. track
   d. intelligence

5. _____ theory suggests that people learn the techniques and attitudes of crime from close relationships with criminal peers.
   a. Social learning
   b. Social process
   c. Social control
   d. Social reaction

6. _____ theory suggests that people commit crime when the forces binding them to society are weakened or broken.
   a. Social learning
   b. Social process
   c. Social control
   d. Social reaction

7. _____ theory suggests that people become criminals when labeled as such and when they accept the label as a personal identity.
   a. Social learning
   b. Social process
   c. Social control
   d. Social reaction

8. Which of the following is NOT one of the most prominent forms of social learning theory?
   a. differential neutralization theory
   b. rationalization theory
   c. differential association theory
   d. neutralization theory

9. According to Sutherland, acquiring a behavior is a _____ process.
   a. psychological
   b. political
   c. legal
   d. social

10. According to Sutherland, skills and motives conducive to crime are learned as a result of contact with _____.
    a. pro-crime values
    b. strain
    c. the American dream
    d. genetic predisposition

11. The conflict of social attitudes and cultural norms is the basis for the concept of _____.
    a. differential neutralization
    b. labeling
    c. differential association
    d. self control

12. Differential association may vary in
    a. frequency, duration, sophistication and context.
    b. duration, frequency, priority, and intensity.
    c. priority, intensity, context and elevation.
    d. intensity, sophistication, frequency and duration.

13. According to differential association theory, the following are ideas that prohibit crime except
    a. play fair.
    b. the end justifies the mean.
    c. don't be a bully.
    d. forgive and forget.

14. According to differential association theory, the following are ideas that justify crime except
    a. drinking is ok.
    b. don't let anyone push you around.
    c. I don't get even, I get mad.
    d. turn the other cheek.

15. Movement in and out of delinquency, shifting between conventional and deviant values is known as
    a. shift.
    b. drift.
    c. slide.
    d. slip.

16. According to Sykes and Matza, the technique of neutralization that is used when young offenders sometimes claim that their unlawful acts are not their fault but from forces beyond their control or accident is referred to as
    a. denial of responsibility.
    b. denial of injury.
    c. denial of victim.
    d. condemnation of the condemners.

17. According to Sykes and Matza, the technique of neutralization that is used when offenders claim that the victim "had it coming" is referred to as
    a. denial of responsibility.
    b. denial of injury.
    c. denial of victim.
    d. condemnation of the condemners.

18. According to Sykes and Matza, the technique of neutralization that is used when offenders view the world as a corrupt place and they are no worse than those in authority such as police and judges who are corrupt is referred to as
    a. denial of responsibility.
    b. denial of injury.
    c. denial of victim.
    d. condemnation of the condemners.

19. Learning theories help explain the important role that _____ play in shaping criminal and conventional behaviors.
    a. sports figures
    b. family
    c. television characters
    d. strangers

20. Early versions of control theory speculated that criminality was a product of
    a. strong self-concept.
    b. weak self-concept.
    c. weak temperament.
    d. good self-esteem.

21. According to social process theory, law violating behavior is the product of
    a. poor human development and culturalization.
    b. genetic weaknesses and chemical imbalances.
    c. free will and well conceived plots.
    d. the capitalist system and institutional anomie.

22. Which of the following statements is TRUE regarding the socialization process?
    a. Children from two parent families are more likely to engage in criminal activity than those from single-parent families.
    b. Delinquent youths tend to have high levels of self-control.
    c. Television has the most dramatic impact on likely juvenile delinquency.
    d. Individuals are strongly influenced by those relationships that are intimate and personal.

23. Which of the following seems to have the LEAST effect on shaping criminality via the socialization process?
    a. labeling
    b. free will
    c. social bonds
    d. neutralization

24. Which of the following statements supports social process theories?
    a. Children from broken-homes have lower rates of criminality versus those from two parent families.
    b. Fraternal twins have higher rates of criminality than identical twins.
    c. Individuals who attend religious services regularly commit less crime than those who do not.
    d. Children with ADHD commit more crime than those who do not.

25. While your previous anti-social behavior went relatively unnoticed your recent norm violation has come to the attention of your parents and police who now label you a "troublemaker." This is the onset of
    a. primary deviance.
    b. secondary deviance.
    c. first-degree criminality.
    d. second-degree criminality

26. When someone rationalizes deviant behavior in order to temporarily drift into it, he is utilizing
    a. diversion practices.
    b. neutralization techniques.
    c. deviance reduction strategies.
    d. conformity separations.

27. Which of the following statements is FALSE according to social process theories?
    a. All people have the potential of becoming criminal.
    b. IQ is the prime determinant of criminality.
    c. Being labeled can lead to stigmatization and greater criminality.
    d. People learn criminal behavior much as they learn any other behavior.

28. _____ occurs when a negative label has a long-term effect on a person's self-image and social interactions.
    a. Stigmatization
    b. Conformity
    c. Drift
    d. Neutralization

29. _____ permits an offender to pay restitution or perform community service rather than face the stigma of a formal trial.
    a. Reflected appraisal
    b. Labeling
    c. Contrition
    d. Diversion

30. _____ programs are a product of the social process perspective.
    a. Boot Camp
    b. Three-strikes
    c. Head Start
    d. Mandatory sentencing

True/False

1. T / F Family relationships are NOT considered a major determinant of behavior.

2. T / F High self-esteem is inversely related to criminal behavior.

3. T / F Adolescents who do NOT receive affection from their parents during childhood are more likely to use illicit drugs and be more aggressive as they mature.

4. T / F Children growing up in homes where a parent suffers mental impairment are also at risk for delinquency.

5. T / F Children whose parents abuse drugs are not more likely to become persistent substance abusers than the children of non-abusers.

6. T / F Children who experience abuse, neglect, or sexual abuse are believed to be more crime prone.

7. T / F Children who fail in school are no more likely to offend than those who do not fail in school.

8. T / F Actually attending religious services has a more dramatic effect on behavior than merely holding religious beliefs.

9. T / F Educational failure has not been linked to criminality.

10. T / F Social learning assumes that people are born bad and must be controlled in order to be good.

11. T / F Culture conflict results from exposure to opposing norms, attitudes and differences of right and wrong.

12. T / F Stigmatization is the result of an application of a negative label with enduring effects on a person's self-image and social interactions.

13. T / F Attachment involves the time, energy, and effort expended in conventional actions such as getting an education.

14. T / F Attachment refers to a person's ability to neutralize beliefs about right and wrong.

15. T / F In the testing of social control theory, youths who were strongly attached to their parents were more likely to commit criminal acts.

Fill in the Blank

1. Socialization is influenced by _____ and _____.

2. Children who have warm and affectionate ties to their parents report greater levels of _____ beginning in adolescence and extending into their adulthood.

3. Children who grow up in homes where parents use severe discipline yet lack warmth and involvement in their lives are prone to _____ behavior.

4. Schools contribute to criminality by _____ problem youths, which sets them apart from conventional society.

5. Religion binds people together and forces them to confront the _____ of their behavior.

6. Social learning theories assume that people are born _____ and learn to be _____.

7. _____ theory assumes that whether good or bad, people are controlled by the evaluations of others.

8. _____ theory assumes that people commit crime when their social learning leads them to perceive more definitions favoring crime than favoring conventional behavior.

9. People experience what Sutherland calls _____ when they are exposed to opposing attitudes toward right and wrong or moral and immoral.

10. Control theorist Walter Reckless argues that a strong _____ insulates a youth from the pressures of criminogenic influences in the environment.

11. The ties that bind people to society, including relationships with friends, family, neighbors, teachers, and employers is referred to as _____.

12. According to Hirschi, social control is measured by a person's _____, _____, _____, and _____.

13. Social reaction theory, also known as _____ theory, explains criminal careers in terms of destructive social interactions and stigma-producing encounters.

14. Negative labels _____ people and reduce their self-image.

15. Howard Becker refers to people who create rules as _____.

Essay

1. Explain the basic principles of differential association.

   - Criminal behavior is learned and is a by-product of interacting with others.

   - Criminal techniques are learned.

   - Criminals are exposed to attitudes and norms in opposition to conventional values.

   - Differential associations vary in frequency, duration, intensity and priority.

2. Discuss the testing and analysis of differential association theory.

   Research is supportive of the core principles.

   - Crime is intergenerational.

   - People who have attitudes supportive of criminal behavior are more likely to engage in criminal behavior.

   - Having delinquent friends or romantic partner increases likely criminality.

   - Kids that associate with aggressive peers are more likely to be aggressive.

   - There is cross-national support.

3. Discuss the basics of neutralization theory.

    - People use justifications for engaging in criminal behavior.

    - Criminals sometimes feel guilt.

    - Often admire law abiding citizens.

    - Define their victims.

    - Not immune to some conformity.

4. Discuss the main elements of contemporary social control theory.

    - Criminality is tied to weakened social bonds. Strong bonds are supported by:

        o   Attachment to others.

        o   Commitment (time and energy) to conventional behavior

        o   Belief in conventional norms.

        o   Involvement in conventional activities.

5. Discuss the basis of social reaction theories.

    - Destructive social interactions and stigmatizing producing encounters.

    - Behaviors deemed criminal are subjective.

    - Crime is defined by those in power.

    - People can be labeled both positively and negatively.

    - Labeling can lead to differential treatment by others and subsequently stigmatization.

ANSWER KEY FOR CHAPTER REVIEW QUESTIONS

Multiple Choice

1.	(c) parental efficacy	p. 148
2.	(b) social process	p. 147
3.	(a) do poorly in school	pp. 148-149
4.	(c) track	pp. 148-149
5.	(a) social learning	p. 150
6.	(c) social control	p. 150
7.	(d) social reaction	p. 150
8.	(b) rationalization theory	p. 150
9.	(d) social	p. 150
10.	(a) pro-crime values	p. 150
11.	(c) differential association	p. 150
12.	(b) duration, frequency, priority, and intensity	p. 152
13.	(b) the end justifies the means	p. 154
14.	(d) turn the other cheek	p. 154
15.	(b) drift	p. 154
16.	(a) denial of responsibility	p. 154
17.	(c) denial of victim	p. 154
18.	(d) condemnation of the condemners	p. 154
19.	(b) family	p. 148
20.	(b) weak self concept	p. 158
21.	(a) poor human development and culturalization	pp. 147-148
22.	(d) relationships that are intimate and personal	p. 152
23.	(b) free will	p. 149
24.	(c) Those who attend religious services commit less crime.	p. 164
25.	(b) secondary deviance	p. 164
26.	(b) neutralization techniques	p. 154-155
27.	(b) IQ is the prime determinant of criminality.	p. 147
28.	(a) stigmatization	pp. 162-163
29.	(d) Diversion	p. 169
30.	(c) Head Start	p. 168

True/False

1. False   p. 148
2. True   p. 158
3. True   p. 148
4. True   p. 148
5. False   p. 148
6. True   p. 148
7. True   p. 148
8. True   p. 150
9. False   p. 148
10. False   p. 159
11. True   p. 154
12. False   p. 162
13. False   p. 158-159
14. False   pp. 158-159
15. False   p. 154

Fill in the Blank

1. key social processes; institutions   p. 141
2. self-esteem   p. 158
3. antisocial   p. 148
4. labeling   p. 162
5. consequences   p. 164
6. good; bad   pp. 147-148
7. social reaction   p. 150
8. Differential association   p. 150
9. culture conflict   p. 150
10. self image   p. 158
11. social bonds   p. 158
12. attachment; commitment; involvement; belief   pp. 158-159
13. labeling   p. 150
14. stigmatize   p. 162
15. moral entrepreneurs   p. 162

Essay

1. pp. 150-154
2. pp. 153-154
3. pp. 154-156
4. pp. 157-162
5. pp. 163-163

8 Social Conflict Theory: It's a Class Thing

LEARNING OBJECTIVES

After mastering the content of this chapter, a student should be able to:

1. Understand the concept of social conflict and how it shapes behavior.
2. Discuss elements of conflict in the justice system.
3. Explain the idea of critical criminology.
4. Discuss the difference between structural and instrumental Marxism.
5. Discuss the various techniques of critical research.
6. Discuss the term left realism.
7. Understand the concept of patriarchy.
8. Explain what is meant by feminist criminology.
9. Discuss peacemaking.
10. Understand the concept of restorative justice.

KEY WORDS AND DEFINITIONS

Radical or Marxist criminology - The view that crime is a product of the capitalist system. p. 174

Power - The ability of persons and groups to control the behavior of others, to shape public opinion, and to define deviance. p. 176

Surplus value - The difference between what workers produce and what they are paid, which goes to business owners as profits. p. 178

Marginalization - Displacement of workers, pushing them outside the economic and social mainstream. p. 178

Globalization - The process of creating a global economy through transnational markets and political and legal systems. p. 179

Instrumental theory – A view that sees criminal law and the criminal justice system as capitalist instruments for controlling the lower class. p. 180

Structural theory – An idea based on the belief that criminal law and the criminal justice system are means of defending and preserving the capitalist system. p. 180

Demystify - To unmask the true purpose of law, justice, or other social institutions. p. 181

Left realism - Approach that sees crime as a function of relative deprivation under capitalism and favors pragmatic, community-based crime prevention and control. p. 184

Preemptive deterrence - Efforts to prevent crime through community organization and youth involvement. p. 185

Critical feminism - Approach that explains both victimization and criminality among women in terms of gender inequality, patriarchy, and the exploitation of women under capitalism. p. 185

Patriarchal - Male-dominated. p. 185

Paternalistic families - Father is breadwinner and rule maker; mother has menial job or is homemaker only. Sons are granted greater freedom than daughters. p. 187

Role exit behaviors - Strategies such as running away or contemplating suicide used by young girls unhappy with their status in the family. p. 187

Egalitarian families - Husband and wife share similar positions of power at home and in the workplace. Sons and daughters have equal freedom. p. 187

Power–control theory - The view that gender differences in crime are a function of economic power (class position, one- versus two-earner families) and parental control (paternalistic versus egalitarian families). p. 187

Peacemaking - Approach that considers punitive crime control strategies to be counterproductive and favors the use of humanistic conflict resolution to prevent and control crime. p. 188

Restorative justice - Using humanistic, non-punitive strategies to right wrongs and restore social harmony. p. 189

Sentencing circle - A peacemaking technique in which offenders, victims, and other community members are brought together in an effort to formulate a sanction that addresses the needs of all. p. 191

CHAPTER SUMMARY

Social conflict theorists view crime as a function of the conflict that exists in society. Conflict theorists suggest that crime in any society is caused by class conflict. Laws are created by those in power to protect their rights and interests. All criminal acts have political undertones. Richard Quinney has called this concept "the social reality of crime." One of conflict theory's most important premises is that the justice system is biased and designed to protect the wealthy. Crime, they contend, is a political concept.

Marxist criminology views the competitive nature of the capitalist system as a major cause of crime. The poor commit crimes because of their frustration, anger, and need. The wealthy engage in illegal acts because they are used to competition and because they must do so to keep their positions in society. Marxist scholars have attempted to show that the law is designed to protect the wealthy and powerful and to control the poor, have-not members of society. Among the branches of critical theory are instrumental Marxism and structural Marxism. The former holds that those in power wield their authority to control society and keep the lower classes in check. The latter maintains that the justice system is designed to maintain the status quo and is used to punish the wealthy if they bend the rules governing capitalism.   Left realism argues, however, that critical criminologists fail to take into account that it is the lower class that is also the victims and need protection.

Research on critical theory focuses on how the system of justice was designed and how it operates to further class interests. Quite often, this research uses historical analysis to show how the capitalist classes have exerted control over the police, courts, and correctional agencies. Both critical and conflict criminology have been heavily criticized by consensus criminologists, who suggest that social conflict theories make fundamental errors in their concepts of ownership and class interest. New forms of social conflict theory have been emerging.

Feminist writers draw attention to the influence of patriarchal society on crime. According to power–control theory, gender differences in the crime rate can be explained by the structure of the family in a capitalist society. Left realism takes a centrist position on crime by showing its rational and destructive nature; the justice system is necessary to protect the lower classes until a socialist society can be developed, which will end crime. Postmodern theory looks at the symbolic meaning of law and culture. Peacemaking criminology brings a call for humanism to criminology. Conflict principles have been used to develop the restorative justice model. This holds that reconciliation rather than retribution should be used to prevent and control crime.

CHAPTER OUTLINE

I. The Origins of Critical Criminology

    A. Contemporary Critical Criminology

II. How Critical Criminologists Define Crime

III. How Critical Criminologists View the Cause of Crime

    A. Globalization

IV. Instrumental v. Structural Theory

    A. Instrumental Theory

    B. Structural Theory

V. Research on Critical Criminology

    A. PROFILES IN CRIME: Mumia Abu Jamal

VI. Critique of Critical Criminology

VII. Emerging Forms Critical Criminology

    A. Left Realism

    B. Critical Feminist Theory

    C. Peacemaking Criminology

VIII. Critical Theory and Public Policy

    A. The Concept of Restorative Justice

    B. The Process of Restoration

    C. Restoration Programs

    D. Balanced and Restorative Justice (BARJ)

    E. POLICY AND PRACTICE IN CRIMINOLOGY

    F. The Challenge of Restorative Justice

CRITICAL THINKING QUESTIONS

1. Critical criminology is aimed at identifying "real crime" such as sexism and racism. Do you share this perspective? Why? Why not?

2. Would you consider tougher immigration laws as racist and an attack on the poor?

3. Find crime statistics for Japan. Are they low or high? What does that say about critical criminology's contention that capitalism causes crime.

4. Can you find a society that is considered matriarchal? What is its crime rate?

CHAPTER REVIEW QUESTIONS

Multiple Choice

1. The view that crime is a product of the capitalist system is the basis of
    a. social structure criminology.
    b. Marxist criminology.
    c. biological criminology.
    d. sociological criminology.

2. Chambliss and Seidman documented how the justice system protects the
    a. poor.
    b. underclass.
    c. minority.
    d. powerful.

3. Feminist scholars critically analyze
    a. gender.
    b. race.
    c. genetics
    d. neighborhoods.

4. Critical criminologists view crime as a function of the _____ mode of production.
    a. capitalist
    b. communist
    c. socialist
    d. agrarian

5. Those in power use _____ as a tool to maintain their control over society.
    a. public schools
    b. religious organizations
    c. the fear of crime
    d. the welfare system

6. The poor are controlled through
    a. unemployment.
    b. incarceration.
    c. death.
    d. hunger.

7. Those who see criminal law and the criminal justice system as capitalist instruments for controlling the lower class are referred to as _____ Marxists.
    a. Instrumental
    b. Structural
    c. Marginalized
    d. Deterrence

8. Those who believe that criminal law and the criminal justice system are means of defending and preserving the capitalists system are referred to as _____ Marxists.
   a. Instrumental
   b. Structural
   c. Marginalized
   d. Neutralizing

9. Instrumental Marxists consider it essential to _____ law and justice.
   a. create
   b. intensify
   c. allocate
   d. demystify

10. The difference between what workers produce and what they are paid, which goes to business owners as profits, is known as
    a. marginalization.
    b. globalization.
    c. surplus value.
    d. mechanization.

11. Displacement of workers, pushing them outside the economic and social mainstream is known as
    a. marginalization.
    b. globalization.
    c. surplus value.
    d. mechanization.

12. The process of creating a global economy through transnational markets and political and legal systems is known as
    a. marginalization.
    b. globalization.
    c. surplus value.
    d. mechanization.

13. Critical theory research is all of the following EXCEPT
    a. humanistic.
    b. situational.
    c. rigid.
    d. descriptive.

14. Recent developments in the conflict approach include all of the following EXCEPT
    a. legal realism.
    b. Biopsychology.
    c. feminist theory.
    d. power-control theory.

15. Preemptive deterrence is an effort to prevent crime through
    a. community disorganization.
    b. youth involvement.
    c. community organization.
    d. Youth avoidance.

16. According to Marxist feminism, the exploitation of women is done by
    a. everyone.
    b. mothers.
    c. husbands.
    d. sisters.

17. A male-dominated social system is referred to as
    a. patriarchal.
    b. matriarchal.
    c. monarchal.
    d. a dictatorship.

18. According to Messerschmidt, capitalist society is utilized by men to
    a. elevate the status of women.
    b. "control the power surplus."
    c. "do gender."
    d. lower the crime rates.

19. Power-control theory claims that crime and delinquency are a function of
    a. class position, fear and social structure.
    b. power, matriarchy and strain.
    c. family functions, psychodynamics and development.
    d. Class position, power and control.

20. _____ families are characterized by the father as breadwinner and rule-maker and the mother has a menial job or serves as the homemaker.
    a. Paternalistic
    b. Maternalistic
    c. Monarchist
    d. Anarchist

21. According to social conflict the, law violating behavior is the product of
    a. poor parenting.
    b. genetic engineering.
    c. careful thought and planning.
    d. the unequal distribution of wealth and power.

22. Which of the following statements is TRUE according to social conflict theorists?
    a. Criminality results from social inequality.
    b. Public spending on the poor is adequate.
    c. Street criminals are more likely to be wealthy than poor.
    d. Crime is a product of socialism.

23. According to feminist theory, which of the following seems to have the LEAST effect on shaping criminality and structuring crime?
    a. age
    b. socio-economic status
    c. opportunity
    d. race

24. Which of the following statements supports rational choice theory?
    a. Drug users and dealers rarely attempt to conceal their behavior.
    b. Even serial killers use cunning and thought to avoid detection.
    c. People who cannot control their hormones commit most crime.
    d. Burglars prefer to rob crowded house, rather than empty ones.

25. Women commit less crime according to radical feminists because
    a. they are less genetically predisposed.
    b. the patriarchic society limits their opportunities to offend.
    c. they are less likely to live in a capitalist country.
    d. they have a "humanist" approach to criminality.

26. Marxist theorize that the primary cause of crime is
    a. socialism.
    b. communism.
    c. fascism.
    d. capitalism.

27. _____ are insulated from street crime because they live far removed from it.
    a. African Americans
    b. The poor
    c. The rich
    d. The homeless

28. The peacemaking technique in which offenders, victims, and other community members are brought together in an effort to formulate a sanction that addresses the needs of all is called a
    a. prosecution pow wow.
    b. sentencing circle.
    c. community jury.
    d. penal panel.

29. The sentencing outcome for radical criminologists is focused on
    a. deterrent justice.
    b. retributional justice.
    c. restorative justice.
    d. incapacitory justice.

30. According to Marxists,
    a. crime is a result of socialism.
    b. crime is determinant.
    c. crime is deviant.
    d. crime is a political concept.

True/False

1. T / F The ability of persons and groups to control the behavior of others, to shape public opinion, and to define deviance is referred to as bullying.

2. T / F According to conflict theory, definitions of crime favor those who control the justice system

3. T / F Research on conflict theory reveals that both white and black offenders have been found to receive stricter sentences if their personal characteristics show them to be members of the "dangerous classes."

4. T / F Critical criminologists are supportive of military build ups and cuts in social programs.

5. T / F Marginalization occurs when workers are pushed out of the economic and social mainstream.

6. T / F Marx identified the economic structures in society that control all human relations. Marx planted the seeds of critical criminology.

7. T / F According to critical criminology, crimes of the helpless such as burglary and robbery are expressions of rage over unjust conditions.

8. T / F According to critical criminology, modern global capitalism helps destroy the lives of workers in less developed countries.

9. T / F All societies have consistent ways of dealing with criminal behavior.

10. T / F Iraq is known for practicing restorative justice.

11. T / F Left realists feel that police are wrongly accused of much of the police brutality citizens complain about.

12. T / F Restorative justice programs must be aware of the cultural and social differences within the United States.

13. T / F In egalitarian families, the husband and wife share similar positions of authority.

14. T / F According to restorative justice principles, victims and the schools are central to justice processes.

15. T / F According to restorative justice principles, the first priority of justice processes is to assist the police.

Fill in the Blank

1. According to conflict theory, laws are created and enforced by those in _____ to protect their own interests.

2. Social conflict theory describes how power relations create _____ in U.S. society.

3. The _____ calls for a humanist version of justice.

4. The conflict definition of crime states that crime is a _____ concept designed to protect the power and position of the upper classes at the expense of the poor.

5. Instrumental Marxists' goal for criminology is to show how capitalist law preserves _____ power.

6. In a patriarchal system, women's work is _____.

7. Because women work within the household and in the labor market, they produce far greater _____ for capitalists than men.

8. According to Messerschmidt, the struggle of men to dominate women in order to prove their manliness is called _____.

9. _____ are the strategies such as running away or contemplating suicide used by young girls unhappy with their status in the family.

10. Peacemakers view the efforts of the state to punish and control as crime-_____ rather than crime-_____.

11. Peacemakers advocate _____ and _____ rather than _____ and _____.

12. _____ uses humanistic, nonpunitive strategies to right wrongs and restore social harmony.

13. _____ is an approach that explains both victimization and criminality among women in terms of gender inequality.

14. _____ view criminal law and the criminal justice system as capitalist instruments for controlling the lower class.

15. Each society produces its own type and amount of _____.

Essay

1. Briefly discuss the branches of social conflict theory as depicted on p. 175 of your textbook.

   - Social Conflict

   - Critical Criminology

   - Emerging fields

        o Critical

        o Power-control

        o Post-modern

        o Peacekeeping

2. Discuss how conflict theorists view globalization of the world's economy as a threat.

   - Surplus value

   - Skirting environmental laws

   - Outsourcing

   - New "imperialism"

        o Spread of capitalism and inequality.

        o Vulnerability of indigenous peoples.

        o Growth of international financial institutions.

        o Non-democratic operation of financial institutions.

3. Discuss the research on critical criminology including the critiques.

   - Rarely uses the scientific method.
   - Prefer to examine historical trends and patterns.
     - Increased punishment to protect wealth (England)
   - Has used empirical research to show the effects of race in shaping criminal justice system decisions.
     - Police enforcement
     - Sentencing
     - Distribution of punishment
   - Critiques
     - Arguments are not new and ignore social and environmental factors.
     - Neglects the fact that capitalist systems correct themselves.
     - Fail to address problems in socialist and communist countries and very low crime rates in some capitalist countries.

4. How would critical feminist theory explain the violent abuse of women by men.

   - Inequality of power between men and women in capitalist society.
     - Men use power to dominate economically and biologically (patriarchy).
     - Women are marginalized.
     - Powerlessness leads to victimization.
     - Men are taught to be aggressive toward women.

5. Explain the main points of Balance and Restorative Justice.

   - Hold offenders accountable to victims.
   - Rehabilitate offenders to re-enter society.
   - Ensure community safety.

ANSWER KEY FOR CHAPTER REVIEW QUESTIONS

Multiple Choice

1.	(b) Marxist criminology	p. 171
2.	(d) powerful	p. 176
3.	(a) gender	p. 185
4.	(a) capitalist	pp. 174-175
5.	(c) the fear of crime	p. 178
6.	(b) incarceration	p. 177
7.	(a) Instrumental	p. 180
8.	(b) Structural	p. 180
9.	(d) demystify	p. 181
10.	(c) surplus value	p. 178
11.	(a) marginalization	p. 179
12.	(b) globalization	p. 178
13.	(c) rigid	pp. 176-178
14.	(b) biopsychology	pp. 174-175
15.	(b) youth involvement	p. 185
16.	(c) husbands	p. 185
17.	(a) patriarchal	p. 185
18.	(c) "do gender"	p. 186
19.	(d) class position, power and control	p. 187
20.	(a) Paternalistic	p. 187
21.	(d) the unequal distribution of wealth and power.	p. 178
22.	(d) Criminality results from social inequality	pp. 178-179
23.	(d) race	p. 185
24.	(b) role exit behavior	p. 187
25.	(a) the patriarchic society limits opportunities to offend.	p. 185
26.	(d) capitalism	p. 178
27.	(c) The rich	p. 178
28.	(b) sentencing circle	p. 191
29.	(c) restorative justice	p. 189
30.	(a) crime is a political concept	pp. 176-177

True/False

1. False   p. 176
2. True   p. 176
3. True   pp. 176-177
4. False   p. 177
5. True   p. 179
6. True   p. 173
7. True   p. 174
8. True   p. 178
9. False   p. 177
10. False   p. 192
11. False   p. 184
12. True   p. 194
13. True   p. 187
14. False   p. 189
15. False   p. 189

Fill in the Blank

1. power   p. 176
2. inequities   p. 178
3. peacemaking movement   p. 188
4. Preemptive deterrence   p. 185
5. ruling-class   p. 176
6. patriarchal   p. 185
7. surplus value   p. 178
8. doing gender   p. 176
9. Role exit behavior   p. 187
10. encouraging; discouraging   pp. 188-189
11. mediation; conflict resolution; punishment; prison   pp. 188-189
12. restorative justice   p. 189
13. Critical feminism   p. 184
14. Instrumental theorists   pp. 180-181
15. crimes   p. 177

Essay

1. pp. 174-177
2. pp. 179-180
3. pp. 181-184
4. pp. 185-186
5. pp. 193-194

9 Developmental Theories: Things Change... Or Do They?

LEARNING OBJECTIVES

After mastering the content of this chapter, a student should be able to:

1. Explain the concept of developmental theory.
2. Identify the factors that influence the life course.
3. Recognize that there are different pathways to crime.
4. Discuss what is meant by "problem behavior syndrome."
5. Differentiate between "adolescent-limited" and "life-course persistent" offenders.
6. Understand the "turning points in crime."
7. Discuss the influence of social capital on crime.
8. Discuss what is meant by a latent trait.
9. Describe the concepts of impulsivity and self control.
10. Discuss Gottfredson and Hirschi's general theory of crime.

KEY WORDS AND DEFINITIONS

Developmental theory - The view that criminality is a dynamic process, influenced by social experiences as well as individual characteristics. p. 198

Latent trait theory - The view that criminal behavior is controlled by a "master trait," present at birth or soon after, that remains stable and unchanging throughout a person's lifetime. p. 199

Life course theory - Theory that focuses on changes in criminality over the life course; developmental theory. p. 199

Problem behavior syndrome (PBS) - A cluster of antisocial behaviors that may include family dysfunction, substance abuse, smoking, precocious sexuality and early pregnancy, educational underachievement, suicide attempts, sensation seeking, and unemployment, as well as crime. p. 200

Authority conflict pathway- Pathway to criminal deviance that begins at an early age with stubborn behavior and leads to defiance and then to authority avoidance. p. 201

Covert pathway - Pathway to a criminal career that begins with minor underhanded behavior, leads to property damage, and eventually escalates to more serious forms of theft and fraud. p. 201

Overt pathway - Pathway to a criminal career that begins with minor aggression, leads to physical fighting, and eventually escalates to violent crime. p. 201

Human capital - What a person or organization actually possesses. p. 202

Adolescent-limited - Offender who follows the most common criminal trajectory, in which antisocial behavior peaks in adolescence and then diminishes. p. 202

Life course persister - One of the small groups of offenders whose criminal career continues well into adulthood. p. 203

Turning points - Critical life events, such as career and marriage, that may enable adult offenders to desist from crime. p. 204

Social development model (SDM) - A developmental theory that attributes criminal behavior patterns to childhood socialization and pro- or antisocial attachments over the life course. p. 205

Prosocial bonds - Socialized attachment to conventional institutions, activities, and beliefs. p. 205

Interactional theory - A developmental theory that attributes criminal trajectories to mutual reinforcement between delinquents and significant others over the life course—family in early adolescence, school and friends in mid-adolescence, and social peers and one's own nuclear family in adulthood. p. 205

Social capital - Positive relations with individuals and institutions, as in a successful marriage or a successful career, that support conventional behavior and inhibit deviant behavior. p. 205

Latent trait - A stable feature, characteristic, property, or condition, such as defective intelligence or impulsive personality, that makes some people crime prone over the life course. p. 210

General theory of crime (GTC) - A developmental theory that modifies social control theory by integrating concepts from biosocial, psychological, routine activities, and rational choice theories. p. 211

Antisocial potential (AP) - An individual's potential to commit antisocial acts. p. 212

CHAPTER SUMMARY

The basis of developmental theory is the view that criminality is a dynamic process, influenced by social experiences as well as individual characteristics. Latent trait theories hold that some underlying condition present at birth or soon after controls behavior. Suspect traits include low IQ, impulsivity, and personality structure. This underlying trait explains the continuity of offending because, once present; it remains with a person throughout his or her life.

People with latent traits choose crime over non-crime; the opportunity for crime mediates their choice. Life course theories argue that events that take place over the life course influence criminal choices. The cause of crime constantly changes as people mature. At first, the nuclear family influences behavior; during adolescence, the peer group dominates; in adulthood, marriage and career are critical. There are a variety of pathways to crime: some kids are sneaky, others hostile, and still others defiant. The general theory of crime, developed by Gottfredson and Hirschi, integrates choice theory concepts.

Crime may be part of a variety of social problems, including health, physical, and interpersonal troubles. The social development model finds that living in a disorganized area helps weaken social bonds and sets people off on a delinquent path. According to interactional theory, crime influences social relations, which in turn influences crime; the relationship is interactive. The sources of crime evolve over time. Problem behavior syndrome contends that criminality is just one factor in a cluster of antisocial behaviors that may include family dysfunction, substance abuse, smoking, precocious sexuality and early pregnancy, educational underachievement, suicide attempts, sensation seeking, and unemployment, as well as crime.

Sampson and Laub's age-graded theory holds that the social sources of behavior change over the life course. People who develop social capital are best able to avoid antisocial entanglements. Important life events or turning points enable adult offenders to desist from crime. Among the most important are getting married and serving in the military. According to David Farrington's ICAP theory, people with antisocial potential (AP) stand a greater chance of engaging in criminal offenses and remaining in a life of crime.

CHAPTER OUTLINE

I.   Foundations of Developmental Theory

II. Life-Course Fundamentals

    A. Problem Behavior Syndrome

    B. Pathways to Crime

        1. Authority Conflict Pathway

        2. Covert Pathway

        3. Overt Pathway

    C. Offense Specialization/Generalization

    D. Age of Onset/Continuity of Crime

    E. Adolescent-Limiteds and Life-Course Persisters

III. Theories of Criminal Life Course

    A. Sampson and Laub's Age-Graded Theory

        1. Social Capital

        2. Turning Points

        3. Testing Age-Graded Theory

        4. The Marriage Factor

        5. Future Research Direction

    B. CURRENT ISSUES IN CRIME: Tracking Down the 500 Delinquent Boys in the New Millennium

IV. Latent Trait Theories

    A. Crime in Human Nature

    B. General Theory of Crime

        1. The Act and the Offender

        2. Impulsivity and Crime?

        3. Self-Control and Crime

        4. Support for GTC

     5. Analyzing the General Theory of Crime
- a) tautological
- b) different classes of criminals
- c) ecological differences
- d) racial and gender differences
- e) moral beliefs
- f) peer influence
- g) people change
- h) modest relationship
- i) cross-cultural difference
- j) misreads human nature
- k) one of many causes
- l) more than one kind of impulsivity
- m) not all criminals are impulsive

  C. CURRENT ISSUES IN CRIME: Careers in the Drug Trade

V. Public Policy Implications of Developmental Theory

CRITICAL THINKING QUESTIONS

1. Search the news for a juvenile arrested for a violent offense. What does the case suggest about his/her prosocial bonds?

2. Can you think of any important "turning points" besides marriage and career? What are they?

3. You have been assigned to help a group of teens identified with a "master trait" of low self-control. What type of approach would you use to help reduce their likelihood to engage in criminal behavior.

4. Ask your friends if they have engaged in any criminal behavior. Do they continue to do so, or have most of the "desisted?" Ask them what factor affected their change in behavior?

CHAPTER REVIEW QUESTIONS

Multiple Choice

1. _____ theory is the view that criminality is a dynamic process, influenced by social experiences as well as individual characteristics.
   a. Developmental
   b. Latent trait
   c. Life course
   d. Problem behavior

2. _____ theory is the view that criminal behavior is controlled by a "master trait."
   a. Developmental
   b. Latent trait
   c. Life course
   d. Problem behavior

3. _____ is the view that focuses on changes in criminality over the life course.
   a. Developmental theory
   b. Latent trait theory
   c. Life course theory
   d. Problem behavior syndrome

4. According to developmental theory, marriage and military service are _____ factors that can explain the onset and continuation of criminality.
   a. personal
   b. social
   c. socialization
   d. cognitive

5. According to developmental theory, information processing and attention/perception are _____ factors that can explain the onset and continuation of criminality.
   a. personal
   b. social
   c. socialization
   d. cognitive

6. Which of the following is not one of the criticisms directed at GTC?
   a. tautological
   b. personality disorder
   c. cross-cultural differences
   d. poor methodology

7. The GTC claims that _____ personality is key.
   a. weak
   b. strong
   c. psychotic
   d. impulsive

8. An offender who follows the most common criminal trajectory, in which antisocial behavior peaks in adolescence and then diminishes, is referred to as
   a. adolescent-limited.
   b. life course persister.
   c. career criminal.
   d. life-long deviance.

9. Which one of the following is a small group of offenders whose criminal career continues well into adulthood?
   a. adolescent-limiteds
   b. life course persisters
   c. career criminals
   d. long-term deviants

10. According to _____, crime is just one among a group of antisocial behaviors that cluster together.
    a. Social bond.
    b. control theory.
    c. problem behavior syndrome
    d. labeling theory.

11. The characteristic of life course persisters, who tend to engage in early sexuality and drug use is referred to as
    a. prematurity.
    b. immaturity.
    c. pseudomaturity.
    d. aging out.

12. PBS involves all of the following EXCEPT
    a. family dysfunction.
    b. substance abuse.
    c. educational overachievement.
    d. sensation seeking.

13. PBS problem behaviors can be divided into the following forms except _____.
    a. social
    b. biological
    c. environmental
    d. personal

14. The pioneering _____ tracked the onset and termination of criminal careers.
    a. Gorings
    b. Sutherlands
    c. Blaus
    d. Gluecks

15. _____ is the pathway to a criminal career that begins with minor underhanded behavior, leads to property damage, and eventually escalates to more serious forms of theft and fraud.
    a. Authority conflict
    b. Covert
    c. Overt
    d. Aging out

16. _____ is the pathway to a criminal career that begins with minor aggression, leads to physical fighting, and eventually escalates to violent crime.
    a. Authority conflict
    b. Covert
    c. Overt
    d. Aging out

17. _____ is the pathway to criminal deviance that begins at an early age with stubborn behavior and leads to defiance and then to authority avoidance.
    a. Authority conflict
    b. Covert
    c. Overt
    d. Aging out

18. Sampson and Laub identify critical life events, such as career and marriage that may enable adult offenders to desist from crime. These critical life events are known as
    a. event points.
    b. life points.
    c. crime points.
    d. turning points.

19. _____ attributes criminal trajectories to mutual reinforcement between delinquents and significant others over the life course—family in early adolescence, school and friends in mid-adolescence, and social peers.
    a. International theory
    b. Lombrosian theory
    c. Interactional theory
    d. Projectional theory

20. An individual's probability to commit antisocial acts is referred to as
    a. antisocial personality disorder.
    b. behavior potential.
    c. antisocial potential.
    d. propensity disorder.

21. Gottfredson & Hirschi explained individual difference in criminality as a combination of general theory of crime combined the elements of ____ and ____.
    a. self-esteem, social structure
    b. self-esteem, opportunity
    c. self-control, opportunity
    d. self-control, social structure

22. Which of the following may contribute to an individual having a life-course persister?
    a. poor nutrition as a youth
    b. wealthy parents
    c. lack of job opportunities
    d. rap music

23. Which of the following is a "turning point" that has a tendency to reduce anti-social behavior?
    a. moving to a new location
    b. buying a new car
    c. getting married
    d. graduating from middle-school

24. Having a well paying job, a spouse and owning a home all help build _____ which can reduce the likelihood of criminality.
    a. social control
    b. social learning
    c. social structure
    d. social capital

25. Problem behavior syndrome (PBS) suggests, for example, that an individual who exhibits one anti-social or self-destructive behavior is likely to
    a. "age out" of crime.
    b. watch a lot of Sesame Street.
    c. exhibit additional reckless behaviors.
    d. lack life-course indicators.

26. According to developmental theory, one reason people "age out" of crime is that
    a. all of their delinquent early friends age out.
    b. relations developed later in life are more important and likely non-criminal.
    c. technology limits the ability of "old people" to commit crime.
    d. they develop positive behavioral syndrome.

27. Which of the following is TRUE of "Master Traits?"
    a. They are genetic or developed
    b. They are unstable over time
    c. They exist only in minorities
    d. Women are more likely than me to have one.

28. _____ refers to what a person or organization actually possesses.
    a. Saturation stuff
    b. Opportunity goods
    c. Wealth of knowledge
    d. Human capital

29. Which of the following statements is TRUE according to developmental theorists?
    a. Opportunity to commit crime is constant.
    b. There is more than one pathway to crime.
    c. Criminals who desist crime no longer face other risks.
    d. PBS can be easily controlled with genetic engineering.

30. Those individuals who whose criminal careers peak in adolescence and then diminish are called
    a. child actors.
    b. adolescent-limited offenders.
    c. middle-age recidivists.
    d. teenage transitional criminals.

True/False

1. T /F People who carry suspected latent traits are in danger of becoming career criminals.

2. T /F In GTC, the offender and the criminal act are related concepts.

3. T /F Empirical research on GTC finds that people who commit white-collar and workplace crime have the same-level of control as non-offenders.

4. T /F The weakness of the GTC is its scope and breadth.

5. T /F The life course view is that criminality can best be understood as one of many social problems faced by at-risk youth.

6. T /F Those people who exhibit PBS are no more prone to behavior difficulties than the general population.

7. T /F Racism is a social form of PBS problem behavior.

8. T /F There is only one pathway to crime.

9. T /F Life course persisters begin offending late and age out of crime.

10. T /F According to life course theory, the best predictor of future criminality is past criminality.

11. T /F According to SDM, as children mature within their environment, elements of socialization control their developmental process.

12. T /F Interactional theory holds that causal influences are unidirectional.

13. T /F Building social capital supports conventional behavior and inhibits deviant behavior.

14. T /F People with a history of criminal activity who have been convicted of serious offenses reduce the frequency of their offending if they live with spouses and maintain employment while living in the community.

15. T /F Antisocial Personality is only a long-term phenomenon.

Fill in the Blank

1. GTC modifies and redefines some of the principles articulated in Hirschi's _____ theory.

2. Gottfredson and Hirschi trace the root cause of poor self-control to inadequate_____.

3. Impulsive people have _____ self-control and a _____ bond to society.

4. The life course view is that criminality can best be understood as one of many social problems faced by _____ youth.

5. Family dysfunction is a _____ form of PBS problem behaviors.

6. Early sexuality is a _____ form of PBS problem behaviors.

7. _____ exhibit early onset of crime that persists into adulthood.

8. The _____ model is a developmental theory that attributes criminal behavior patterns to childhood socialization and pro- or antisocial attachments over the life course.

9. _____ are the socialized attachment to conventional institutions, activities, and beliefs.

10. _____ theory holds that seriously delinquent youths form belief systems that are consistent with their deviant lifestyle.

11. According to Sampson and Laub, two critical turning points that enable adult offenders to desist from crime are _____ and _____.

12. Wilson and Herrnstein's model assumes that both _____ and _____ traits influence the crime-non-crime choice.

13. Marriage stabilizes people and helps them build _____.

14. GTC has been criticized for being tautological.

15. According to Sampson and Laub's age-graded theory, building social capital and strong social bonds _____ the likelihood of long-term deviance.

Essay

1. Discuss the differences in criminality between "early onset" and "late starter" criminals.

   - Early Onset
     - They engage in truancy, cruelty to animals, and theft.
     - They are more likely to engage in violence.
     - They have a longer duration of criminality.

2. Why are the important environmental elements of PBS?

   - High crime areas
   - Disorganized neighborhoods
   - Racism
   - Exposure to poverty

3. Discuss Tittle's control balance theory.

   - Control one is subject to by others.
   - Control one exerts over someone else.
   - Imbalance leads to crime.

4. Identify which of the life-course pathways is the most threatening.

   - Overt pathway
     - It escalates to aggressive acts.
     - It begins with bullying.
     - Leads to physical fighting
     - Ends with violence.

5. Discuss the importance of the "marriage factor" on reducing crime.

   - Maturity
   - Children
   - Stabilization
   - Social Capital
   - Reduced contact with criminal peers.

ANSWER KEY FOR CHAPTER REVIEW QUESTIONS

Multiple Choice

1.	(a) developmental	p. 198
2.	(b) latent trait	p. 210
3.	(c) life course	p. 199
4.	(c) socialization	p. 198
5.	(d) cognitive	p. 198
6.	(d) poor methodology	pp. 211-213
7.	(d) impulsive	p. 211
8.	(a) adolescent-limited	p. 202
9.	(b) life-course persister	p. 203
10.	(c) problem behavior syndrome	p. 200
11.	(c) pseudomaturity	p. 203
12.	(c) educational overachievement	p. 200
13.	(b) biological	p. 203
14.	(d) Gluecks	p. 211
15.	(b) Covert	p. 201
16.	(c) Overt	p. 201
17.	(a) Authority conflict	p. 201
18.	(d) turning points	p. 204
19.	(c) Interactional	p. 205
20.	(c) antisocial potential	p. 212
21.	(c) self-control, opportunity	pp. 211-215
22.	(a) poor nutrition	p. 203
23.	(c) getting married	p. 204
24.	(d) social capital	p. 205
25.	(c) other reckless behaviors	p. 200
26.	(b) later relations are important and less criminal	p. 210
27.	(a) genetic or developed	p. 199
28.	(d) Human capital	p. 202
29.	(b) There is more than one criminal pathway	p. 201
30.	(b) Adolescent-limited offender	p. 203

True/False

1.	True	p. 199
2.	False	pp. 211-218
3.	False	pp. 211-218
4.	False	pp. 211-218
5.	True	p. 199
6.	False	p. 200
7.	False	p. 200
8.	False	p. 201
9.	False	p. 199
10.	True	p. 203
11.	True	p. 205

12. False   p. 205
13. True   p. 205
14. True   p. 214
15. False   p. 212

Fill in the Blank

1. social control   p. 204
2. child-rearing practices   p. 213
3. low; weak   p. 213
4. self-control   p. 213
5. social   p. 200
6. personal   p. 200
7. Life course persisters   p. 203
8. social development   p. 205
9. Prosocial bonds   p. 205
10. Interactional theory   p. 205
11. career; marriage   p. 204
12. biological, sociological   p. 210-211
13. social capital   pp. 205
14. antisocial potential   p. 212
15. reduces   pp. 204-205

Essay

1. p. 203
2. p. 201
3. p. 212
4. pp. 201-202
5. pp. 207-208

10 Violent Crime

LEARNING OBJECTIVES

After mastering the content of this chapter, a student should be able to:

1. Discuss the various causes of violent crime.
2. Discuss the concept of the brutalization process.
3. Discuss the history of rape.
4. Understand the different types of rape.
5. Discuss the legal issues in rape prosecution.
6. Recognize that there are different types of murder.
7. Discuss the differences between serial killing, mass murder, and spree killing.
8. Understand the nature of assault in the home.
9. Understand the careers of armed robbers.
10. Discuss newly emerging forms of violence such as stalking, hate crimes, and workplace violence.
11. Understand the different types of terrorism and what is being done today to combat terrorist activities.

KEY WORDS AND DEFINITIONS

Eros - The life instinct, which drives people toward self-fulfillment and enjoyment. p. 225

Thanatos - The death instinct, which produces self destruction. p. 225

Psychopharmacological relationship - The direct consequence of ingesting mood-altering substances. p. 226

Economic compulsive behavior - Drug users who resort to violence to support their habit. p. 226

Systemic link - A link that occurs when drug dealers turn violent in their competition with rival gangs. p. 226

Subculture of violence - Violence has become legitimized by the custom and norms of that group. p. 227

Rape - The carnal knowledge of a female forcibly and against her will. p. 228

Date rape - A rape that involves people who are in some form of courting relationship. p. 230

Marital exemption - Traditionally, a legally married husband could not be charged with raping his wife. p. 230

Statutory rape - Sexual relations between an underage minor female and an adult male. p. 230

Virility mystique - The belief that males must separate their sexual feelings from needs for love, respect, and affection. p. 231

Narcissistic personality disorder - A pattern of traits and behaviors that indicate infatuation and fixation with one's self to the exclusion of all others and the egotistic and ruthless pursuit of one's gratification, dominance, and ambition. p. 231

Aggravated rape - Rape involving multiple offenders, weapons, and victim injuries. p. 232

Consent - The victim of rape must prove that she in no way encouraged, enticed, or misled the accused rapist. p. 232

Shield laws - Laws that protect women from being questioned about their sexual history unless it directly bears on the case. p. 233

Murder - The unlawful killing of a human being with malice aforethought. p. 233

First-degree murder - Killing a person after premeditation and deliberation. p. 233

Premeditation - Considering the criminal act beforehand, which suggests that it was motivated by more than a simple desire to engage in an act of violence. p. 233

Deliberation - Planning a criminal act after careful thought rather than carrying it out on impulse. p. 233

Felony murder - A killing accompanying a felony, such as robbery or rape. p. 234

Second-degree murder - A person's wanton disregard for the victim's life and his or her desire to inflict serious bodily harm on the victim, which results in the victim's death. p. 234

Manslaughter - Homicide without malice. p. 234

Voluntary or nonnegligent manslaughter - A killing committed in the heat of passion or during a sudden quarrel that provoked violence. p. 234

Involuntary or negligent manslaughter - A killing that occurs when a person's acts are negligent and without regard for the harm they may cause others. p. 234

Infanticide - A murder involving a very young child. p. 235

Eldercide - A murder involving a senior citizen. p. 235

Serial killer - A person who kills more than one victim over a period of time. p. 237

Mass murderer - A person who kills many victims in a single, violent outburst. p. 239

Spree killer - A killer of multiple victims whose murders occur over a relatively short span of time and follow no discernible pattern. p. 239

Battery - Offensive touching, such as slapping, hitting, or punching a victim. p. 239

Assault - Does not require actual touching but involves either attempted battery or intentionally frightening the victim by word or deed. p. 239

Road rage - Violent assault by a motorist who loses control while driving. p. 240

Child abuse - Any physical or emotional trauma to a child for which no reasonable explanation, such as an accident or ordinary disciplinary practices, can be found. p. 241

Neglect - Not providing a child with the care and shelter to which he or she is entitled. p. 241

Child sexual abuse - The exploitation of children through rape, incest, and molestation by parents or other adults. p. 241

Robbery - Taking or attempting to take anything of value from the care, custody, or control of a person or persons by force or threat of force or violence and/or by putting the victim in fear. p. 242

Acquaintance robbery - A robber whose victims are people he or she knows. p. 244

Hate or bias crimes - Violent acts directed toward a particular person or members of a group merely because the targets share a discernible racial, ethnic, religious, or gender characteristic. p. 245

Workplace violence - Violence such as assault, rape, or murder committed at the workplace. p. 247

Stalking - A course of conduct directed at a specific person that involves repeated physical or visual proximity, nonconsensual communication, or verbal, written, or implied threats sufficient to cause fear in a reasonable person. p. 248

Terrorism - Premeditated, politically motivated violence perpetrated against noncombatant targets by subnational groups or clandestine agents, usually intended to influence an audience. p. 248

International terrorism - Terrorism involving citizens or the territory of more than one country. p. 248

Terrorist group - Any group practicing, or that has significant subgroups that practice, international terrorism. p. 248

Death squads - The use of government troops to destroy political opposition parties. p. 251

USA Patriot Act (USAPA) - An act that gives sweeping new powers to domestic law enforcement and international intelligence agencies in an effort to fight terrorism, to expand the definition of terrorist activities, and to alter sanctions for violent terrorism. p. 253

CHAPTER SUMMARY

Violence has become an all too common aspect of modern life. Among the various explanations for violent crimes are the availability of firearms, human traits, a subculture of violence that stresses violent solutions to interpersonal problems, and family conflict. There is also a strong connection between drug and alcohol abuse and crime.

Rape, the carnal knowledge of a female forcibly and against her will, has been known throughout history, but society's view of rape has evolved. Causes of rape include evolutionary factors, male socialization, psychological abnormalities, social learning and sexual motivation. At present, close to 100,000 rapes are reported to U.S. police each year; the actual number of rapes is probably much higher. However, like other violent crimes, the rape rate is in decline. There are numerous forms of rape including statutory, acquaintance, and date rape. Rape is an extremely difficult charge to prove in court. The victim's lack of consent must be proven; therefore, it almost seems that the victim is on trial. Traditionally, a legally married husband could not be charged with raping his wife. Consequently, changes are being made in rape law and procedure. Rape shield laws have been developed to protect victims from having their personal life placed on trial.

Murder is defined as killing a human being with malice aforethought. There are different degrees of murder, and punishments vary accordingly. First degree murder is the most serious and requires premeditation and deliberation on the part of the perpetrator. Like rape, the murder rate and the number of annual murders is in decline. Manslaughter is a category for homicides without malice. Murder can involve a single victim or be a serial killing, mass murder, or spree killing that involves multiple victims. Women commit only a small portion of all murders. One important characteristic of murder is that the victim and criminal often know each other. Murder often involves an interpersonal transaction in which a hostile action by the victim precipitates a murderous relationship.

Assault and battery are serious interpersonal violent crimes and often occurs in the home, including child abuse, parent abuse, and spouse abuse. Assault does not require actual touching but involves either attempted battery or intentionally frightening the victim by word or deed. Battery involves offensive touching, such as slapping, hitting, or punching a victim. The demographics of assaults mirror those of murder and tend to be intraracial, and involve young males. There also appears to be a trend toward violence between dating couples. Robbery involves theft by force, usually in a public place. Robbery is considered a violent crime because it can and often does involve violence. Robbers often target acquaintances. Newly emerging forms of violent crime include hate crimes, stalking, and workplace violence. Hate or bias crimes are violent acts directed toward a particular person or members of a group merely because the targets share a discernible racial, ethnic, religious, or gender characteristic. Roots of hate crimes include thrill-seeking, reactive violence, mission and retaliatory attacks.

Terrorism is a significant form of violence. Many terrorist groups exist at both the national and international levels. There are a variety of terrorist goals including political change, nationalism, causes, criminality, and environmental protection. Terrorists may be motivated by criminal gain, psychosis, grievance against the state, or ideology. The FBI and the Department of Homeland Security have been assigned the task of protecting the nation from terrorist attacks. The USA Patriot Act was passed to provide them with greater powers.

CHAPTER OUTLINE

I.   The Causes of Violence
   A.   Personal Traits
   B.   Ineffective Families
   C.   Evolutionary Factors/Human Instinct
       1.   Eros
       2.   Thanatos
   D.   Exposure to Violence
   E.   Substance Abuse
       1.   A psychopharmacological relationship
       2.   Economic compulsive behavior
       3.   A systematic link
   F.   Firearm Availability
   G.   Cultural Values
   H.   National Values

II. Forcible Rape
  A. Incidence of Rape
  B. Types of Rapists
    1. Power
    2. Anger
    3. Sadistic
  C. Types of Rape
    1. Date rape
    2. Marital rape
    3. Statutory rape
  D. The Causes of Rape
    1. Evolutionary, biological factors
    2. Male socialization
      a) virility mystique
    3. Psychological abnormality
      a) narcissistic personality disorder
    4. Social learning
    5. Sexual motivation
  E. Rape and the Law
    1. Proving rape
    2. Consent
    3. Legal reform
      a) Shield laws
III. Murder and Homicide
  A. Degrees of Murder
    1. First-degree Murder
      a) premeditation
      b) deliberation
    2. Second-degree murder
    3. Homicides
      a) Manslaughter
        (1) Voluntary or non-negligent
        (2) Involuntary or negligent
  B. The Nature and Extent of Murder
  C. Murderous Relations
    1. Romantic Relations
    2. Personal Relations
    3. Stranger Relations
    4. Student Relations

D. Serial Killers, Mass Murderers, and Spree Killers

    1. Serial Killers

        a) Thrill Killers

        b) Mission Killers

        c) Expedience Killers

    2. Female Serial Killers

    3. Mass Murderers

        a) Revenge killers

        b) Love killers

        c) Profit killers

        d) Terrorists killers

    4. Spree Killers

E. PROFILES IN CRIME: The Angel of Death

IV. Assault and Battery

A. Nature and Extent of Assault

B. Domestic Violence: Assault in the Home

    1. Child Abuse

        a) Child sexual abuse

    2. Causes of Child Abuse

    3. Parental Abuse

    4. Spousal Abuse

V. Robbery

A. The Armed Robber

B. Acquaintance Robbery

VI. Emerging Forms of Interpersonal Violence

A. Hate Crimes

    1. Roots of Hate

        a) Thrill-seeking

        b) Reactive

        c) Mission

        d) Retaliatory

    2. Nature and Extent of Hate Crimes

    3. Controlling Hate Crime

    4. Free Speech?

B. Workplace Violence

C. Stalking

VII. Terrorism

    A. Contemporary Forms of Terrorism

        1. Revolutionary Terrorists

        2. Political Terrorists

        3. Nationalist Terrorism

        4. Caused-Based Terrorism

        5. Environmental Terrorism

        6. State-Sponsored Terrorism

        7. Criminal Terrorism

    B. CONTEMPORARY ISSUES IN CRIME: Transnational Terrorism in the New Millennium

    C. What Motivates Terrorists?

    D. PROFILES IN CRIME: Osama Bin Laden

    E. Responses to Terrorism

CRITICAL THINKING QUESTIONS

1. It is generally accepted that there is a systematic link between drugs and crime. Sample the crime stories in your local newspaper. Of the crimes reported, what percentage suggest a drug-crime connection?

2. Go to the FBI's website and review their 10 most wanted list. What types of crimes are most represented? Why do you suppose that is the case? Would you add someone to that list?

3. There are various types of terrorists identified in your text. Find statistics on the web that show which type presents the greatest risk to your safety?

4. Frequent exposure to violent images may increase violent behavior. Are you constantly exposed to such images in video games, television etc. How often? Do you feel it has any influence on your behavior?

CHAPTER REVIEW QUESTIONS

Multiple Choice

1. Killing a person after premeditation and deliberation is
   a. first degree murder.
   b. felony murder.
   c. second-degree murder.
   d. manslaughter.

2. A killing committed in the heat of passion or during a sudden quarrel that provoked violence is
   a. first degree murder.
   b. felony murder.
   c. second-degree murder.
   d. manslaughter.

3. A killing accompanying a felony, such as robbery or rape is
   a. first degree murder.
   b. felony murder.
   c. second-degree murder.
   d. manslaughter.

4. Homicide without malice is
   a. first degree murder.
   b. felony murder.
   c. second-degree murder.
   d. manslaughter.

5. More than _____ of the homicides occur in cities with a population of 100,000 or more.
   a. one quarter
   b. half
   c. three quarters
   d. 90 percent

6. Murder victims tend to be primarily
   a. females.
   b. males.
   c. elderly.
   d. juveniles.

7. The life instinct, which drives people toward self-fulfillment and enjoyment is called
   a. eros
   b. thanatos
   c. menthos
   d. cantos

8. A person who kills more than one victim over a period of time is known as a
   a. serial killer.
   b. mass murderer.
   c. spree killer.
   d. macho killer.

9. A killer of multiple victims whose murders occur over a relatively short span of time and follow no discernable pattern is known as a
   a. serial killer.
   b. mass murderer.
   c. spree killer.
   d. mucho murderer

10. A person who kills many victims in a single, violent outburst is known as a
    a. serial killer.
    b. mass murderer.
    c. spree killer.
    d. Mucho murdere.

11. The types of mass murderers include all of the following EXCEPT
    a. revenge killers.
    b. love killers.
    c. thrill killers.
    d. profit killers.

12. The types of serial killers include all of the following except
    a. thrill killers.
    b. mission killers.
    c. expedience killers.
    d. revenge killers.

13. Female serial killers possess education levels that are
    a. above average.
    b. average.
    c. below average.
    d. extremely minimal.

14. A _____ relationship may be the result of the ingesting of mood-altering substances.
    a. pseudo-developmental
    b. neo-developmental
    c. psychopharmaceutical
    d. hypoallergenic

15. The NCVS indicates that only about _____ of all serious assaults are reported to the police.
    a. one quarter
    b. one half
    c. two-thirds
    d. three-quarters

16. A grown man who engages in sexual behavior with an underage girl would be guilty of
    a. eros battery.
    b. marital sexual assault.
    c. sexual robbery.
    d. statutory rape.

17. _____ robbers focus on stealing from people they know.
    a. Friendship
    b. Family
    c. Acquaintance
    d. Colleagues

18. Robbers use _____ to steal which separates them from thieves.
    a. stealth
    b. cunning
    c. force
    d. drugs

19. Suspected causes of rape include the socialization process called
    a. regicide.
    b. women's intuition.
    c. the biological determinant.
    d. the virility mystique.

20. The Earth Liberation Front is an example of a _____ terrorist group.
    a. environmental
    b. state-sponsored
    c. revolutionary
    d. nationalist

21. When someone vents anger, frustration or rage by sexually assaulting a woman, he is categorized as a _____ rapist.
    a. anger
    b. sadistic
    c. power
    d. sophisticated

22. Which of the following is true of most patterns of violent crimes?
    a. They occur in winter
    b. They involve knives
    c. They occur between acquaintances
    d. They occur in rural areas

23. How strong is the link between pornography and rape?
    a. Very strong
    b. Modest
    c. Weak
    d. This relationship is not supported.

24. One idea of why rape persists is that
    a. men do not have others alternatives to sexual gratification.
    b. historically women have been viewed as "spoils of conquest."
    c. as society has changed, women wear more provocative clothing.
    d. rape no longer exists as a crime problem.

25. Why is it often difficult to get a conviction in an "acquaintance rape" case?
    a. There is no DNA available.
    b. Police do not take rape claims seriously unless there is serious violence.
    c. Defense attorneys can raise a defendant's past sexual history.
    d. Both parties may likely have been intoxicated resulting in "he said/she said."

26. There are an estimated _____ violent acts on school grounds each year.
    a. 18,000
    b. 150,000
    c. 740,000
    d. 1,280,000

27. Which is a contributing factor to increasing the likelihood of someone becoming a spousal abuser?
    a. having been a battered child
    b. having been a concentric youth
    c. possessing the spousal abuse gene
    d. possessing large amounts of pornography

28. _____ was created as part of the Patriot Act.

    a. The FBI
    b. The CIA
    c. The Bureau of Immigration Defense
    d. The Department of Homeland Security

29. _____ is the death life instinct that drives people toward risk-taking.
    a. Ego
    b. Eros
    c. Thantos
    d. Menthos

30. _____is the murder of an older child.
    a. Infanticide
    b. Filicide
    c. Regicide
    d. Patricide

True/False

1. T / F Almost half of homicides occur in cities with a population of less than 10,000.

2. T / F Murderers tend to be males.

3. T / F The older the child, the greater the risk for infanticide.

4. T / F Although highly publicized in the media, the average annual incidence of school shootings is very small.

5. T / F Kids who have been the victims of crime themselves are the ones most likely to bring guns to school.

6. T / F The BTK killer is an example of a spree-killer.

7. T / F Male serial killers are almost always substance abusers.

8. T / F Battery does not require actual touching for it to occur.

9. T / F Assault involves intentionally frightening the victim by word or deed.

10. T / F It is difficult to estimate the actual number of child abuse cases because many incidents are never reported to the police.

11. T / F Women who were abused as children are at no greater risk to be re-abused as adults than those women who did not experience abuse as children.

12. T / F Revolutionary terrorists primarily promote the interest of people or political minority group.

13. T / F Robberies seem to peak during the winter months.

14. T / F The FBI was created to combat international terrorism.

15. T / F Hate crimes usually involve convenient, vulnerable targets who are incapable of fighting back.

Fill in the Blank

1. Planning a criminal act after careful thought rather than carrying it out on impulse is referred to as _____.

2. Considering the criminal act beforehand, which suggests that it was motivated by more than a simple desire to engage in an act of violence, is referred to as _____.

3. A murder involving a very young child is known as _____.

4. A murder involving a senior citizen is known as _____.

5. Serial killer males _____ their victims before attacking, while serial killer females _____ their victims to their deaths.

6. The _____ is an important legislative response to the attacks of 9-11.

7. Not providing a child with the care and shelter to which he or she is entitled in referred to as _____.

8. Parents are sometimes the target of abuse from _____.

9. Excessive _____ use may turn otherwise docile husbands into wife abusers.

10. _____ terrorists direct violence at people or groups who oppose their ideology. The KKK is an example.

11. _____ are violent acts directed toward a particular person or members of a group merely because the targets share a discernible racial, ethnic, religious, or gender characteristic.

12. Perpetrators of _____ hate crimes rationalize their behavior as a defensive stand taken against outsiders whom they believe threaten their community or way of life.

13. A difficulty in stopping hate crime results from the _____ protections of even groups like the KKK.

14. Violence such as assault, rape, or murder committed at one's job is known as _____.

15. _____ is a course of conduct directed at a specific person that involves repeated physical or visual proximity, nonconsensual communication, or verbal, written, or implied threats sufficient to cause fear in a reasonable person.

Essay

1. How do murderous relations develop between two people who may have had little prior conflict?

    -   Romantic Relations

    -   Personal Relations

    -   Stranger Relations

    -   Student Relations

2. Discuss the types of rapists.

    -   Anger

    -   Power

    -   Sadistic

3. Discuss the factors in child-to-parent violence (CPV).

    -   The younger the child the more CPV

    -   More assaults on mothers than fathers.

    -   Both boys and girls hit mothers more than fathers.

    -   Slightly more boys than girls hit parents.

    -   Associated with parent-parent violence, corporal punishment and child abuse.

4. Discuss why acquaintance robbery may be attractive for a number of rational reasons.

    -   Victims are reluctant to report the crime.

    -   Some robberies are motivated by street justice.

    -   Robber knows it will be a good "take."

    -   Desperation may lead to robbery of those in close proximity.

5. Discuss the potential motivations for hate crimes.

    -   Thrill-seeking

    -   Reactive

    -   Mission

    -   Retaliatory

ANSWER KEY FOR CHAPTER REVIEW QUESTIONS

Multiple Choice

1.	(a) first degree murder	p. 233
2.	(e) voluntary manslaughter	p. 233
3.	(b) felony murder	p. 233
4.	(d) manslaughter	p. 233
5.	(b) half	p. 233
6.	(b) males	p. 233
7.	(a) eros	p. 225
8.	(a) serial killer	p. 237
9.	(c) spree killer	p. 239
10.	(b) mass murderer	p. 239
11.	(c) thrill killers	p. 237
12.	(d) revenge killers	p. 238
13.	(c) below average	p. 239
14.	(c) psychopharmaceutical	p. 226
15.	(b) one half	p. 240
16.	(d) statutory rape	pp. 230-231
17.	(c) Acquaintance robbery	p. 244
18.	(c) force	p. 242
19.	(d) virility mystique	p. 231
20.	(a) national terrorist	p. 248
21.	(a) anger	p. 228
22.	(c) They occur between acquaintances.	p. 235
23.	(d) No link has been established.	p. 231
24.	(b) Women are viewed as spoils of war.	p. 228
25.	(d) Often a he "said/she said" situation.	pp. 232-233
26.	(c) 740,000	p. 237
27.	(a) having been a battered child	p. 241
28.	(d) The Department of Homeland Security	p. 222
29.	(c) Thantos	p. 225
30.	(a) Infanticide	p. 253

True/False

1.	False	p. 234
2.	True	p. 234
3.	False	p. 235
4.	True	pp. 236-237
5.	True	pp. 236-237
6.	False	p. 237
7.	False	p. 238
8.	False	p. 239
9.	True	p. 239
10.	True	p. 241
11.	False	p. 241
12.	False	p. 249

13. True   p. 243
14. False   p. 253
15. True   p. 245

Fill in the Blank

1. deliberation   p. 233
2. premeditation   p. 233
3. infanticide   pp. 236-237
4. eldercide   pp. 236-237
5. track; lure   p. 239
6. Patriot Act   p. 253
7. neglect   pp. 241-242
8. their own children   p. 242
9. alcohol use   p. 242
10. political   p. 249
11. Hate crimes   p. 245
12. Reactive   pp. 245-246
13. free speech   p. 247
14. workplace violence   p. 247
15. Stalking   p. 248

Essay

1. p. 235-237
2. p. 230
3. p. 242
4. pp. 244-245
5. pp. 245-246

11 Property Crimes

LEARNING OBJECTIVES

After mastering the content of this chapter, a student should be able to:

1. Understand the history of theft offenses.
2. Recognize the differences between professional and amateur thieves.
3. Explain the similarities and differences between the different types of larceny.
4. Understand the different forms of shoplifting.
5. Discuss the concept of fraud.
6. Explain what is meant by a confidence game.
7. Understand what it means to burgle a home.
8. Discuss what it takes to be a "good burglar."
9. Understand the concept of arson.
10. Discuss why people commit arson for profit.

KEY WORDS AND DEFINITIONS

Occasional criminals - Offenders who do not define themselves by a criminal role or view themselves as committed career criminals. p. 259

Situational inducement - Short-term influence on a person's behavior, such as financial problems or peer pressure, that increases risk-taking. p. 259

Professional criminals - Offenders who make a significant portion of their income from crime. p. 260

Larceny - Taking for one's own use the property of another, by means other than force or threats on the victim or forcibly breaking into a person's home or workplace; theft. p. 260

Constructive possession - A legal fiction that applies to situations in which persons voluntarily give up physical custody of their property but still retain legal ownership. p. 261

Petit (petty) larceny - Theft of a small amount of money or property, punished as a misdemeanor. p. 261

Grand larceny - Theft of money or property of substantial value, punished as a felony. p. 261

Shoplifting - The taking of goods from retail stores. p. 262

Booster - Professional shoplifter who steals with the intention of reselling stolen merchandise. p. 263

Snitch - Amateur shoplifter who does not self identify as a thief but who systematically steals merchandise for personal use. p. 263

Merchant privilege laws - Legislation that protects retailers and their employees from lawsuits if they arrest and detain a suspected shoplifter on reasonable grounds. p. 264

Target removal strategy - Displaying dummy or disabled goods as a means of preventing shoplifting. p. 264

Target hardening strategy - Locking goods into place or using electronic tags and sensing devices as means of preventing shoplifting. p. 264

Naive check forgers - Amateurs who cash bad checks because of some financial crisis but have little identification with a criminal subculture. p. 267

Systematic forgers - Professionals who make a living by passing bad checks. p. 267

False pretenses or fraud - Misrepresenting a fact in a way that causes a deceived victim to give money or property to the offender. p. 267

Confidence game - A swindle, usually involving a get-rich quick scheme, often with illegal overtones, so that the victim will be afraid or embarrassed to call the police. p. 268

Fence - A receiver of stolen goods. p. 269

Embezzlement - Taking and keeping the property of others, such as clients or employers, with which one has been entrusted. p. 271

Burglary - Entering a home by force, threat, or deception with intent to commit a crime. p. 271

Arson - The willful, malicious burning of a home, building, or vehicle. p. 275

CHAPTER SUMMARY

Economic crimes are designed to financially reward the offender. Opportunistic amateurs commit the majority of economic crimes such as shoplifting. Economic crime has also attracted professional criminals. Professionals earn most of their income from crime, view themselves as criminals, and possess skills that aid them in their law-breaking behavior. A good example of the professional criminal is the fence who buys and sells stolen merchandise.

Common theft offenses include larceny, fraud, and embezzlement. These are common-law crimes, originally defined by English judges. Self-reports suggest that a significant number of juveniles have engaged in theft. Larceny involves taking the legal possessions of another. Larceny amounts are set by each state, but petty larceny is typically theft of amounts under $100; grand larceny usually refers to amounts over $100. Larceny is the most common theft crime and involves such activities as shoplifting, passing bad checks, stealing, or illegally using credit cards. Some shoplifters (snitches) are amateurs who steal on the spur of the moment, but others are professionals (boosters) who use sophisticated techniques to help them avoid detection. Merchant privilege laws are an attempt to protect retailers and their employees from lawsuits if they arrest and detain a suspected shoplifter on reasonable grounds.

The crime of false pretenses, or fraud, is similar to larceny in that it involves the theft of goods or money; it differs in that the criminal tricks victims into voluntarily giving up their possessions. Embezzlement involves people taking something that was temporarily entrusted to them, such as bank tellers taking money out of the cash drawer and keeping it for themselves. Confidence games involve swindle and stings usually involving a get-rich quick scheme, often with illegal overtones, so that the victim will be afraid or embarrassed to call the police. Auto theft usually involves amateur joyriders who "borrow" cars for short-term transportation and professional auto thieves who steal cars to sell the parts that are highly valuable.

Burglary, a more serious theft offense, was defined in common law as the "breaking and entering of a dwelling house of another in the nighttime with the intent to commit a felony within. This definition has also evolved over time. Today most states have modified their definitions of burglary to include theft from any structure at any time of day. Because burglary involves planning and risk, it attracts professional thieves. The most competent have technical competence and personal integrity, specialize in burglary, are financially successful, and avoid prison sentences. Professional burglars are able to size up the value of a particular crime and balance it off with the perceived risks. Many have undergone training in the company of older, more experienced burglars. They have learned the techniques to make them "good burglars." Arson is another serious property crime. Although most arsonists are teenage vandals, others are professional arsonists who specialize in burning commercial buildings for profit.

CHAPTER OUTLINE

I. History of Theft

II. Contemporary Thieves

III. Larceny/Theft

    A. PROFILES IN CRIME: Invasion of the Body Snatchers

    B. Common Larceny/Theft Offenses

    C. Shoplifting

        1. The Shoplifter

           a) boosters

           b) snitches

        2. Controlling Shoplifters

           a) merchant privilege

           b) target removal strategies

           c) target hardening strategies

    D. Credit Card Theft

    E. Auto Theft

        1. Types of Auto Theft

           a) joyriding

           b) short-term transportation

           c) long-term transportation

           d) profit

           e) commission of another crime

        2. Combating auto theft

    F. Bad Checks

    G. False Pretenses/Fraud

    H. Confidence Games

    I. Receiving and Fencing Stolen Property

    J. CURRENT ISSUES IN CRIME: Confessions of a Dying Thief

    K. Embezzlement

IV. Burglary
    A. The Nature and Extent of Burglary
    B. Types of Burglaries
        1. Residential Burglar
        2. Commercial Burglars
        3. Repeat Burglars
    C. Careers in Burglary

V. Arson

CRITICAL THINKING QUESTIONS

1. Apply your text's definition of a confidence game/con to the film *Ocean's 11*. How does that movie show the various elements of a complex criminal enterprise.

2. Check your local newspaper for a burglary in your area. Was it the work of a professional burglar? What factors helped you draw that conclusion?

3. Pretend you are a professional fence. What types of merchandise would you fence? Why? Any merchandise you would refuse to accept? Why?

4. Walk through a parking lot at your university. Make a note of how many automobiles are in the top ten stole vehicles list. How many possess other expensive parts that make them at high risk of theft? Share you findings with the class.

CHAPTER REVIEW QUESTIONS

Multiple Choice

1. By the 18th century, _____ moved freely is sparsely populated areas and transported goods, such as spirits, gems, gold, and spices, without paying tax or duty.
    a. skilled thieves
    b. smugglers
    c. poachers
    d. shoplifters

2. _____ make a significant portion of their income from crime.
    a. Professional criminals
    b. Career criminals
    c. Occasional criminals
    d. Shoplifters

3. Occasional property crime occurs when there is _____ to commit crime.
    a. professional
    b. opportunity
    c. situational inducement
    d. cognitive dissonance

4. Auto thieves often steal _____ which can be worth up to $3,000 per car.
   a. headlights
   b. radiators
   c. brake pads
   d. hood ornaments

5. The amount of theft from businesses has _____ in the past two decades.
   a. decreased slightly
   b. increased slightly
   c. increased dramatically
   d. decreased dramatically

6. Larceny includes _____ larceny.
   a. miniscule and supersized
   b. petit and grand
   c. gross and specious
   d. tiny and majestic

7. English judges created the concept of constructive possession to get around the element of
   a. forgery.
   b. trespassing.
   c. theft.
   d. trespass in the taking.

8. Fewer than _____ percent of shoplifting incidents are detected by store employees.
   a. 2
   b. 5
   c. 10
   d. 20

9. Which type of larceny is charged as a misdemeanor?
   a. grand
   b. petit
   c. personal
   d. property

10. Of the millions of property and theft-related crimes that occur each year, most are committed by _____ criminals.
    a. accessible
    b. occasional
    c. professional
    d. developmental

11. _____ involve locking goods into place or having them monitored by electronic systems.
    a. Merchant privilege laws
    b. Target removal strategies
    c. Target hardening strategies
    d. Merchant defense stratgies

12. _____ are the most commonly stolen vehicles in the United States.
    a. 2001 Kia Sportage
    b. 1995 Honda Civic
    c. 1972 Ford Pinto
    d. 1988 Mercedes 300 Coupe

13. In her pioneering study on shoplifters, Cameron found that about _____ percent of all shoplifters were professionals.
    a. 5
    b. 10
    c. 20
    d. 50

14. A person known for buying and selling goods is called a
    a. lifter.
    b. toll-taker.
    c. bridge.
    d. fence.

15. Amateur pilfers are called _____ in thieves' argot.
    a. boosters
    b. snitches
    c. fences
    d. targets

16. A _____ often involves a con game where people are enticed with a "get rich quick" schemes.
    a. triad theft
    b. confidence game
    c. fence building
    d. trust diversion

17. To encourage the arrest of shoplifters, a number of states have passed _____ laws that are designed to protect retailers and their employees from lawsuits stemming from improper or false arrests of suspected shoplifters.
    a. citizen arrest
    b. clerk privilege
    c. merchant privilege
    d. target arrest

18. Lemert found that the majority of check forgers are
    a. amateurs.
    b. systematic forgers.
    c. embezzlers.
    d. opportunistic criminals.

19. _____ is a legal fiction that applies to situations in which persons voluntarily give up physical custody of their property but still retain legal ownership malicious burning of property is termed
    a. Legal embezzlement.
    b. Constructive possession.
    c. Merchant privilege.
    d. Fence rights.

20. The crime of _____ involves misrepresenting a fact in a way that causes a victim to willingly give his or her property to the wrongdoer, who then keeps it.
    a. embezzlement
    b. fraud
    c. larceny
    d. forgery

21. _____ is defined as any willful or malicious burning or attempted burn a dwelling, motor vehicle or aircraft.
    a. Murder
    b. Arson
    c. Rape
    d. Larceny

22. _____ is the most commonly occurring crime.
    a. Murder
    b. Arson
    c. Rape
    d. Larceny

23. Most reported crimes occur
    a. during the winter months of December and January.
    b. during the spring months of March and April.
    c. during the summer months of July and August.
    d. during the fall months October and November.

24. Which is of the following is TRUE regarding how burglars approach their "job?"
    a. They often target acquaintances.
    b. They rarely operate at night.
    c. They tend to be most successful in "White" neighborhoods.
    d. Their partners are generally women.

25. The NCVS reports approximately _____ burglaries in 2003.
    a. 1,000,000.
    b. 2,000,000
    c. 3,000,000
    d. 4,000,000

26. Agreeing to use your contact with a high government official to help change a government policy in return for money equates with
    a. influence peddling.
    b. loan sharking.
    c. schmoozing.
    d. lobbying.

27. The most prolific arsonists are the _____ fire-setters
    a. playing with matches
    b. crying for help
    c. severely disturbed
    d. delinquent

28. Which of the following is a common type of burglar?
    a. chiseler burglar
    b. residential burglar
    c. money launder burglar
    d. stinger burglar

29. _____ make a living passing bad checks.
    a. Money laundering fences
    b. Professional boosters
    c. Embezzlement amateurs
    d. Systematic forgers

30. Which of the following statements is TRUE regarding property crimes?
    a. Theft is a new phenomenon.
    b. Occasional thieves steal at a consistently high rate.
    c. Professional thieves learn their trades and develop specific skills.
    d. Elderly tend to steal more than younger people.

True/False

1. T / F Criminologists suspect that most economic crimes are the work of amateur criminals.

2. T / F Passing bad checks without adequate funds is a form of robbery.

3. T / F The original common-law definition of larceny required a "trespass in the taking."

4. T / F The American colonists created the concept of constructive possession to get around the element of "trespass in the taking."

5. T / F Grand larceny is punished as a felony.

6. T / F Auto theft adds up to more than $8 billion each year.

7. T / F Boosters are professional shoplifters who steal with the intention of reselling stolen merchandise to fences.

8. T / F Criminologists view shoplifters as people who are not likely to reform if apprehended.

9. T / F Embezzlement is entering a home by force, threat, or deception with intent to commit a crime.

10. T / F Long-term transportation is a common reason for auto theft.

11. T / F Almost 90% of all auto theft claims include airbags.

12. T / F Most active burglars avoid occupied residences, considering them high-risk targets.

13. T / F Most active burglars work in groups.

14. T / F Some burglars repeatedly attack the same target, mainly because they are familiar with the layout and protective measures.

15. T / F Most professional burglars are women.

Fill in the Blank

1. Professional theft includes _____, _____, and _____.

2. _____ was one of the earliest common-law crimes created by English judges to define acts in which one person took for his or her own the property of another.

3. Stores small and large lose at least _____ percent of total sales to thieves.

4. The majority of shoplifters are _____.

5. People who buy stolen property are called _____.

6. Professionals who make a living by passing bad checks are referred to as _____.

7. _____ percent of all auto thefts are reported to police.

8. Misrepresenting a fact in a way that causes a deceived victim to give money or property to the offender is referred to as _____.

9. _____ are run by swindlers who aspire to separate a victim from his or her hard earned money.

10. _____ occurs when trusted persons or employees take someone else's property for their own use.

11. _____ is the breaking and entering of a structure in order to commit a felony, typically theft.

12. The willful, malicious burning of a home, building, or vehicle is referred to as _____.

13. _____ typically involves displaying fake merchandise as a means of deterring theft.

14. _____ thieves are opportunistic amateurs who steal because of situational inducements,

15. Successful fences must develop relationships with _____ , sometimes even acting as an informer, in order to avoid arrest.

Essay

1. What does your text say are the categories of professional theft?
   - Picketpocket
   - Confidence games
   - Forger
   - Extortionist
   - Hotel Thief
   - Jewel Thief
   - Shoplifter
   - Sneak Thief

2. Discuss the strategies to combat shoplifting.
   - Merchant Privilege
   - Target Hardening
   - Target removal

3. Discuss the different types of burglars.
   - Residential Burglars
   - Commercial Burglars
   - Repeat Burglars

4. Discuss how auto theft is combated.
   - Increased apprehension.
   - Marking autos
   - Lojack Systems
   - Publicity Campaigns
   - Closed Circuit Television

5. Discuss why the number of people arrested has increased in the past decade.

- More employees are willing to steal.
- Employers are more willing to report theft.
- Law enforcement is more willing to prosecute.

ANSWER KEY FOR CHAPTER REVIEW QUESTIONS

Multiple Choice

1.	(c) poachers	p. 259
2.	(a) Professional criminals	p. 260
3.	(b) opportunity	pp. 259-260
4.	(a) headlights	pp. 266-267
5.	(c) increased dramatically	p. 262
6.	(b) petite and grand	p. 261
7.	(d) trespass in the taking	p. 272
8.	(c) 10	p. 262
9.	(b) petit	p. 261
10.	(b) occasional	p. 259
11.	(c) target hardening strategies	p. 264
12.	(b) 1995 Honda Civic	p. 265
13.	(b) 10	p. 273
14.	(d) fence	p. 269
15.	(b) snitches	p. 263
16.	(b) confidence game	p. 268
17.	(c) merchant privilege	p. 263
18.	(a) amateurs	p. 267
19.	(b) Constructive possession	p. 261
20.	(b) fraud	p. 267
21.	(b) arson	p. 275
22.	(d) Larceny	p. 260
23.	(c) summer months	p. 272
24.	(a) They target acquaintances.	pp. 271-272
25.	(c) embezzlement	p. 271
26.	(c) 3,000,000	pp. 271-272
27.	(c) severely disturbed	pp. 260-261
28.	(b) residential burglar	pp. 271-272
29.	(b) Systematic forgers	p. 267
30.	(c) Professionals learn trades and skills	p. 260

True/False

1. True   pp. 258-260
2. False   p. 267
3. True   p. 261
4. False   p. 261
5. True   p. 261
6. True   p. 261
7. True   p. 263
8. False   p. 262
9. False   p. 271
10. True   p. 266
11. False p. 266
12. True   p. 273
13. True   p. 273
14. True   p. 273
15. False p. 275

Fill in the Blank

1. shoplifting, extortion, forgery   p. 260
2. theft, larceny   p. 260
3. $10,000,000,000   p. 262
4. snitches and pilferers   p. 263
5. fences   p. 269
6. systematic forgers   p. 267
7. 75   p. 265
8. false pretenses or fraud   p. 267
9. confidence games   p. 268
10. embezzlement   p. 271
11. burglary   p. 271
12. arson   p. 275
13. target removal   p. 264
14. Occasional   p. 271
15. law enforcement   p. 269

Essay

1. p. 260
2. pp. 263-264
3. pp. 272-273
4. p. 267
5. p. 271

12 Enterprise Crime: White-Collar Crime, Cyber Crime, and Organized Crime

LEARNING OBJECTIVES

After mastering the content of this chapter, a student should be able to:

1. Understand the concept of enterprise crime.
2. Explain the various types of white-collar crime.
3. Distinguish between the various types of corporate crime.
4. Recognize the extent and various causes of the white-collar crime.
5. Discuss the different approaches to combating white-collar crime.
6. Recognize the forms taken by cyber crime.
7. Describe the methods being used to control cyber crime.
8. List the different types of illegal behavior engaged in by organized crime figures.
9. Describe the evolution of organized crime.
10. Explain how the government is fighting organized crime.

KEY WORDS AND DEFINITIONS

Enterprise crimes - Crimes of illicit entrepreneurship. p. 280

White-collar crime - Illegal activities of people and institutions whose acknowledged purpose is profit through legitimate business transactions. p. 281

Cyber crime - People using the instruments of modern technology for criminal purposes. p. 280

Organized crime - Illegal activities of people and organizations whose acknowledged purpose is profit through illegitimate business enterprise. p. 281

Sting or swindle - A white-collar crime in which people use their institutional or business position to bilk others out of their money. p. 282

Churning - Repeated, excessive, and unnecessary buying and selling of a client's stock. p. 283

Front running - Brokers place personal orders ahead of a large customer's order to profit from the market effects of the trade. p. 283

Bucketing - Skimming customer trading profits by falsifying trade information. p. 283

Insider trading - Using one's position of trust to profit from inside business information. p. 284

Influence peddling - Using one's institutional position to grant favors and sell information to which one's co-conspirators are not entitled. p. 284

Pilferage - Systematic theft of company property. p. 286

Corporate or organizational crime - Powerful institutions or their representatives willfully violate the laws that restrain these institutions from doing social harm or require them to do social good. p. 287

Sherman Antitrust Act - Subjects to criminal or civil sanctions any person "who shall make any contract or engage in any combination or conspiracy" in restraint of interstate commerce. p. 289

Price-fixing - A conspiracy to set and control the price of a necessary commodity. p. 289

Compliance strategies – Method of controlling white-collar crime that rely on the threat of economic sanctions or civil penalties to control potential violators, creating a marketplace incentive to obey the law. p. 293

Information technology (IT) – All forms of technology used to create, store, retrieve, and exchange data in alls its various forms. p. 295

Globalization – The process of creating transnational markets, politics, and legal systems and forming a global economy. p. 295

Cyber theft – Use of computer networks for criminal profits. p. 295

Denial of service attack – Extorting money from internet service users by threatening to prevent them from accessing the service. p. 297

Warez – Refers to efforts of ongoing groups to download and sell copyrighted software in violation of its license. p. 297

Division of markets - Firms divide a region into territories, and each firm agrees not to compete in the others' territories. p. 298

E-tailing fraud – Using the internet to illegally buy or sell merchandise on the internet. p. 300

Identity theft – Using the internet to steal someone's identity and/or impersonate the victim in order to conduct illicit transactions. p. 300

Phishing – Utilizing legitimate looking emails as a means of illegally obtaining a victim's personal information. p. 300

Alien conspiracy theory - The belief, adhered to by the federal government and many respected criminologists, that organized crime is a direct offshoot of a criminal society. p. 303

Mafia - A criminal society that first originated in Italy and Sicily and now controls racketeering in major U.S. cities. p. 303

Racketeer Influenced and Corrupt Organization Act (RICO) - An act that created new categories of offenses in racketeering activity, which it defined as involvement in two or more acts prohibited by 24 existing federal and 8 state statutes. p. 305

Enterprise theory of investigation (ETI) - Model that focuses on criminal enterprise and investigation attacks on the structure of the criminal enterprise rather than on criminal acts viewed as isolated incidents. p. 305

CHAPTER SUMMARY

Enterprise crimes involve criminal acts that twist the legal rules of commercial enterprise for criminal purposes. Enterprise crimes can be divided into three independent yet overlapping categories: white-collar crime, cyber crimes, and organized crime. White-collar crime involves illegal activities of people and institutions whose acknowledged purpose is profit through legitimate business transactions. Cyber crime involves people using the instruments of modern technology for criminal purpose. Organized crime involves illegal activities of people and organizations whose acknowledged purpose is profit through illegitimate business enterprise.

White-collar crimes include stings and swindles involving the use of deception to bilk people out of their money and chiseling customers, businesses, or the government. Surprisingly, many professionals engage in chiseling offenses. Other white-collar criminals use their positions in business and the marketplace to commit economic crimes, including exploitation of position in a company or the government to secure illegal payments, embezzlement and employee pilferage and fraud, client fraud, and influence peddling and bribery. Further, corporate officers sometimes violate the law to improve the position and profitability of their businesses. Their crimes include price-fixing, false advertising, and environmental offenses. So far, little has been done to combat white-collar crimes. Most offenders do not view themselves as criminals and therefore do not seem to be deterred by criminal statutes. Although thousands of white-collar criminals are prosecuted each year, their numbers are insignificant compared with the magnitude of the problem. The government has used various law enforcement strategies to combat white-collar crime. Some involve deterrence, which uses punishment to frighten potential abusers. Others involve economic or compliance strategies attempt to control white-collar crime by relying on the threat of economic sanctions or civil penalties to control potential violators, creating a marketplace incentive to obey the law.

Cyber criminals use emerging forms of technology to commit criminal acts. In some instances, they involve the use of technology to commit common-law crimes such as fraud and theft. In other instances, the technology itself is the target, for example, illegal copying and sale of computer software and identity theft. Some emerging areas of cyber –crimes are warez—downloading and selling copyrighted material---and, e-tailing---using the internet to illegally buy and sell merchandise on the internet. Millions of people receiving "phishing" emails. Emails that look legitimate, but are attempts to illegally obtain a victim's personal information. Law enforcement officials fear that the incidence of cyber crime will explode in the future.

Organized crime supplies alcohol, gambling, drugs, prostitutes, and pornography to the public. It is immune from prosecution because of public apathy and because of its own strong political connections. Organized criminals used to be white ethnics—Jews, Italians, and Irish—but today African Americans, Hispanics, Russians and Chinese have become involved in organized crime activities. A growing area is the trafficking in humans, and "sex tourism." The old-line "families" are now more likely to use their criminal wealth and power to buy into legitimate businesses. There is debate over the control of organized crime. Some experts view organized crime as a group of disorganized, competing gangs dedicated to extortion or to providing illegal goods and services. Others believe a national crime cartel controls all activities. The enterprise theory of investigation focuses on criminal enterprise and investigation attacks on the structure of the criminal enterprise rather than on criminal acts viewed as isolated incidents. Efforts to control organized crime have been stepped up. The federal government has used antiracketeering statutes to arrest syndicate leaders. The Racketeer Influenced and Corrupt Organization Act created new categories of offenses in racketeering activity, which it defined as involvement in two or more acts prohibited by 24 existing federal and 8 state statutes. But as long as huge profits can be made, illegal enterprises will continue to flourish.

CHAPTER OUTLINE

I. Enterprise Crime

II. White-Collar Crime

III. Components of White-Collar Crime

    A. Stings and Swindles

    B. Chiseling

        1. Professional Chiseling

        2. Securities fraud

            a) Churning

            b) Front Running

            c) Bucketing

    C. Individual Exploitation of Institutional Position

    D. Influence Peddling and Bribery

        1. Influence Peddling in Government

        2. Influence Peddling in Business

    E. Embezzlement and Employee Fraud

        1. Blue-Collar Fraud

        2. Management Fraud

    F. PROFILES IN CRIME: Tyco, Enron and WorldCom: Enterprise Crime at the Highest Levels

    G. Client Fraud

        1. Health Care Fraud

        2. Tax Evasion

    H. Corporate (Organizational) Crime

IV. Theories White-Collar Crime

    A. Rationalization/Neutralization View

    B. Corporate Culture Theory

    C. Self-Control View

V. White-Collar Law Enforcement Systems

    A. Controlling White-Collar Crime

        1. Compliance Strategies

        2. Deterrence Strategies

    B. Is the Tide Turning?

VI. Cyber Crime

    A. CURRENT ISSUES IN CRIME: Cyber Vandalism: Cyber Crime with Malicious Intent

    B. Computer Fraud

    C. Distributing Illegal Sexual Material

    D. Denial-of-Service Attack

    E. Illegal Copyright Infringement

    F. Internet Securities Fraud

        1. Market Manipulation

        2. Fraudulent Offerings of Securities

        3. Illegal Touting

    G. E-Tailing Fraud

    H. Identity Theft

VII. Controlling Cyber Crime

    A. Cyber Crime and Law Enforcement Agencies

VIII. Organized Crime

    A. Characteristics of Organized Crime

    B. Activities of Organized Crime

    C. The Concept of Organized Crime

    D. Contemporary Organized Crime Groups

    E. RACE, CULTURE, GENDER AND CRIMINOLOGY

IX. Controlling Organized Crime

X. The Future of Organized Crime

CRITICAL THINKING QUESTIONS

1. Apply the elements that define organized crime to your favorite "mafia" movie.

2. Research several different countries and the number and types of organized crime groups exist there. Are there many similarities of differences between the groups?

3. Find a government auction in your area. List what types of items have been seized by the government.

4. Do you consider insider-trading a crime? What would you do if a friend offered you a "hot" stock tip?

CHAPTER REVIEW QUESTIONS

Multiple Choice

    1. _____ involves illegal activities of people and institutions whose acknowledged purpose is profit through legitimate business transactions.
        a. Organized crime
        b. Blue-collar
        c. White-collar crime
        d. Imperative Crime

2. Corporate crime involves various illegal business practices such as
   a. price-fixing.
   b. burglary.
   c. armed robbery.
   d. prostitution.

3. The categories of enterprise crime include all of the following EXCEPT
   a. white-collar crime.
   b. cyber crime.
   c. organized crime.
   d. street crime.

4. Distinguished criminologist _____ first used the phrase white-collar crime to describe the criminal activities of the rich and powerful.
   a. Edwin Sutherland
   b. James Q. Wilson
   c. Sigmund Freud
   d. Robert Merton

5. A type of crime where producers pay radio stations to play songs is called
   a. rock-n-roll.
   b. embezzlement
   c. payola.
   d. spinning.

6. _____ involves people using the instruments of modern technology for criminal purposes.
   a. White collar crime
   b. Cyber crime
   c. Organized crime
   d. Mechanized crime

7. Deception by individuals who use their institutional or business position to bilk people out of their money is an example of which category of white-collar crime?
   a. professional chiseling
   b. stings and swindles
   c. securities fraud
   d. influence peddling and bribery

8. Pharmacists have been known to alter prescriptions or substitute low-cost generic drugs for more expensive name brands. This is an example of which category of white-collar crime?
   a. professional chiseling
   b. stings and swindles
   c. securities fraud
   d. influence peddling and bribery

9. _____ in government occurs when a public officials engage in corruption such as taking bribes, or passing contracts on to friends and family.
   a. Influence peddling
   b. Public professional chiseling
   c. Public churning
   d. Securities fraud

10. All of the following EXCEPT one are examples of securities fraud:
    a. churning
    b. front running
    c. bucketing
    d. morphing

11. _____ refers to the failure of a citizen to report taxes properly, but not of more serious activities such as destroying records.
    a. Positive embezzlement
    b. Tragic omission
    c. Active neglect
    d. Passive neglect

12. Blue-collar employees have been involved in systematic theft of company property. This type of theft is commonly called
    a. bucketing.
    b. churning.
    c. front running.
    d. pilferage.

13. Organized crime includes _____ activities.
    a. truancy
    b. loan sharking
    c. charitable
    d. shoplifting

14. The victims of white-collar crime include
    a. the homeless.
    b. inmates.
    c. the general public.
    d. street criminals

15. A white-collar crime in which people use their institutional or business position to bilk others out of their money is known as a
    a. swindle.
    b. wipe out.
    c. contact.
    d. shake-n-bake.

16. Abusive and deceptive health care practices include all of the following techniques except
    a. ping-ponging.
    b. gang visits.
    c. steering.
    d. driving.

17. The Enron case is an example of
    a. health care fraud.
    b. educational fraud.
    c. management fraud.
    d. internet fraud.

18. Computer crime uses several common techniques. Which of the following is NOT one of these techniques?
    a. the Trojan horse
    b. the salami slice
    c. the logic bomb
    d. the super whammy

19. When this type of computer crime technique is used, an employee sets up a dummy account in the company's computerized records. A small amount is subtracted from each customer's account and added to the thief's account.
    a. the Trojan horse
    b. the salami slice
    c. the logic bomb
    d. the super whammy

20. Most organized crime income comes from
    a. armed robbery.
    b. shoplifting.
    c. narcotics distribution.
    d. legitimate business.

21. Which of the following is TRUE regarding white-collar crime?
    a. Only wealthy people can commit these types of crimes.
    b. Computers are rarely used to commit crimes.
    c. White-collar crime and organized crime are linked because they involve entrepreneurship.
    d. Murder is a common white-collar crime.

22. Which of the following is NOT commonly used in chiseling fraud?
    a. sports memorabilia
    b. bogus auto repairs
    c. celebrity autographs
    d. pornography

23. _____ refers to skimming customer trading profits by falsifying trade information.
    a. Bucketing
    b. Dunking
    c. Churping
    d. Slapping

24. _____ is the repeated, excessive, and unnecessary buying and selling of a client's stock.
    a. Slipping
    b. Churning
    c. Hopping
    d. Dueling

25. _____ refers to efforts of ongoing groups to download and sell copyrighted software in violation of its license.
    a. Spamming
    b. Warez
    c. Phishing
    d. Celeb

26. The process of creating transnational markets, politics, and legal systems and forming a global economy is called
    a. globalization.
    b. idolatry.
    c. migration.
    d. transcendentalism.

27. _____ occurs when someone is forced to pay for a service for which he has a right to.
    a. Enhancement
    b. Suspicion
    c. Exploitation
    d. Regression

28. Who is most likely to commit an influence peddling offense?
    a. a member of Congress
    b. a professional athlete
    c. a doctor
    d. an accountant

29. Which of the following is TRUE regarding cyber-crime?
    a. It rarely involves the internet.
    b. The cost of cyber-crime is not very high.
    c. It is easy for law enforcement to combat.
    d. It often crosses international borders.

30. _____ refers to using the internet to illegally buy or sell merchandise on the internet.
    a. Technological shoplifting
    b. Internet embezzlement
    c. E-tailing fraud
    d. Computer counterfeiting

True/False

1. T / F White-collar crime involves the illegal distribution of legal material.

2. T / F Losses from street crime are higher than for white-collar crime.

3. T / F The RICO statute was designed specifically to go after organized crime.

4. T / F White-collar crimes today represent a range of behaviors involving individuals acting alone and within the context of a business structure.

5. T / F Using one's position of trust to profit from inside business information is referred to as churning.

6. T / F The control of workers' safety is the sole responsibility of the Environmental Protection Agency.

7. T / F Selling illegally obtained merchandize on E-bay is an example of e-tailing fraud.

8. T / F Globalization of markets, politics and legal systems has made international crime more difficult to commit.

9. T / F Tax cheating is a serious crime and a great majority of major tax cheats are prosecuted because the IRS is a strong agent of the federal government.

10. T / F Stings and swindles involve long-term efforts to cheat people out of their money.

11. T / F Warez refers to efforts of ongoing groups to download and sell copyrighted software in violation of its license.

12. T / F Cyber crimes cost consumers billions of dollars each year.

13. T / F The primary goal of organized crime is economic gain.

14. T / F Federal and state governments actually did little to combat organized crime until fairly recently.

15. T / F Russian gangs are not very active in international organized crime such as human trafficking.

Fill in the Blank

1. Crimes of illicit entrepreneurship are referred to as _____ crimes.

2. White-collar crime, cyber crime, and organized crime are linked together because they involve _____.

3. According to the alien conspiracy theory, organized crime is made up of a national syndicate that call themselves _____.

4. In 1970, in an effort to control organized crime, Congress passed the

   _____.

5. An individual convicted under RICO is subject to _____ years in prison and a $25,000 fine.

6. The major enforcement arm against environmental crimes is the _____.

7. Extorting money from internet service users by threatening to prevent them from accessing the service is a _____.

8. A conspiracy to set and control the price of a necessary commodity is referred to as

   _____.

9. _____ is the belief, adhered to by the federal government and many respected criminologists, that organized crime is a direct offshoot of a criminal society

10. _____ theory suggests that some businesses actually encourage employees to cheat or cut corners.

11. All forms of technology used to create, store, retrieve or exchange information in all various forms are called _____.

12. Some corporate executives justify criminal behavior by utilizing _____ techniques such as "all people steal when they get into a tight spot."

13. Cyber crimes use _____ to commit crime.

14. _____ is the act of utilizing legitimate looking emails as a means of illegally obtaining a victim's personal information.

15. The model that focuses on criminal enterprise and investigation attacks on the structure of the criminal enterprise rather than on criminal acts viewed as isolated incidents is called _____.

Essay

1. What are the four types of market conditions prohibited under the Sherman Antitrust Act.

   - Division of Markets
   - Tying Arrangement
   - Group Boycott
   - Price fixing

2. Discuss the forms of denial-of-service-attacks.

   - Attempts to flood a computer network and preventing legitimate network traffic.
   - Attempts to disrupt connections within a computer network.
   - Attempts to prevent particular individuals from accessing a service.
   - Attempts to disrupt service to a specific system or person.

3. Discuss what your text tells us embezzlement and the types of employee fraud.

   - Blue-collar Fraud
   - Management Fraud
   - Client Fraud

      Heath Care Fraud

      Tax Evasion

4. Chiseling takes many forms. Discuss them and provide examples.
   - Professional chiseling
   - Pharmacists
   - Securities Fraud
   - Churning
   - Front running
   - Bucketing

5. Discuss the incidence of white collar crime.
   - 50% of households; 36% of individuals victimized in 2005.
   - 1/3 of all citizens report a white-collar crime in their life-time.
   - Most common white collar crimes are pricing fraud and credit card fraud.
   - Most crimes go unreported.
   - The public believes it is a serious problem.

ANSWER KEY FOR CHAPTER REVIEW QUESTIONS

Multiple Choice

1.	(c) White-collar crime	p. 281
2.	(a) price-fixing	p. 289
3.	(d) street crime	pp. 287-290
4.	(a) Edward Sutherland	p. 281
5.	(c) payola	p. 285
6.	(b) Cyber crime	p. 280
7.	(b) stings and swindles	p. 282
8.	(a) professional chiseling	p. 283
9.	(a) Influence peddling	pp. 284-285
10.	(d) morphing	pp. 283-284
11.	(d) passive neglect	p. 287
12.	(d) pilferage	p. 286
13.	(b) loan sharking	pp. 303-304
14.	(c) general public	pp. 287-292
15.	(a) swindle	p. 282
16.	(d) driving	pp. 283-284
17.	(c) management fraud	p. 286
18.	(d) the super whammy	p. 296
19.	(b) the salami slice	p. 296
20.	(d) narcotics distribution	p. 303
21.	(c) White-collar and organized crime are linked.	p. 281
22.	(d) pornography	p. 283
23.	(a) Bucketing	p. 283
24.	(b) Churning	p. 283
25.	(b) Warez	p. 297
26.	(a) globalization	p. 295
27.	(c) Exploitation	p. 284
28.	(a) a member of Congress	p. 285
29.	(d) It often crosses international borders.	p. 295
30.	(c) E-tailing fraud	p. 300

True/False

1.	True	p. 281
2.	False	p. 281
3.	True	p. 305
4.	True	pp. 287-288
5.	False	p. 283
6.	False	pp. 290-291
7.	True	p. 300
8.	False	p. 295
9.	False	p. 287
10.	True	p. 282
11.	True	p. 297
12.	True	p. 295

13. True   p. 302
14. True   p. 293
15. False   pp. 304-307

Fill in the Blank

1.	enterprise	p. 280
2.	entrepreneurship	pp. 280-281
3.	La Cosa Nostra	p. 302
4.	Organized Crime Control Act	p. 305
5.	20	p. 305
6.	Environmental Protection Agency	p. 291
7.	denial of service attack	p. 291
8.	price-fixing	p. 290
9.	Alien conspiracy theory	p. 303
10.	Corporate culture	p. 292
11.	information technology	p. 295
12.	neutralization	p. 292
13.	technology	p. 280
14.	Phishing	p. 300
15.	Enterprise Theory of Investigation	p. 305

Essay

1. p. 290
2. p. 297
3. pp. 285-286
4. pp. 283-284
5. p. 281-282

13 Public Order Crimes

LEARNING OBJECTIVES

After mastering the content of this chapter, a student should be able to:

1. Discuss the legal cases that define the right to personal sexual relations between consenting adults.
2. Discuss the association between law and morality.
3. Understand what is meant by the terms "moral crusade" and "moral entrepreneur."
4. Understand and discuss some of the most common paraphilias.
5. Discuss what is meant by "obscenity."
6. Understand and discuss the various techniques used to control pornography.
7. Discuss the various types of prostitution.
8. Discuss the history of drug abuse.
9. Discuss the cause of substance abuse.
10. Identify the various drug control strategies.

KEY WORDS AND DEFINITIONS

Public order crime - Behavior that is outlawed because it threatens the general well-being of society and challenges its accepted moral principles. p. 311

Victimless crime - Public order crime that violates the moral order but has no specific victim other than society as a whole. p. 312

Moral entrepreneur - A person who creates moral rules, which thus reflect the values of those in power rather than any objective, universal standards of right and wrong. p. 313

Paraphilia - Bizarre or abnormal sexual practices that may involve nonhuman objects, humiliation, or children. p. 314

Prostitution - The granting of non-marital sexual access for remuneration. p. 328

Pornography - Sexually explicit books, magazines, films, or tapes intended to provide sexual titillation and excitement for paying customers. p. 328

Obscenity - Material that violates community standards of morality or decency and has no redeeming social value. p. 328

Temperance movement - The drive to prohibit the sale of alcohol in the United States, culminating in ratification of the Eighteenth Amendment in 1919. p. 333

Prohibition - The period from 1919 until 1933, when the Eighteenth Amendment to the U.S. Constitution outlawed the sale of alcohol; also known as the "noble experiment." p. 333

Narcotic - A drug that produces sleep and relieves pain, such as heroin, morphine, and opium; a habit-forming drug. p. 338

CHAPTER SUMMARY

Public order crimes are acts considered illegal because they conflict with social policy, accepted moral rules, and public opinion. There is usually great debate over public order crimes. Some charge that they are "victimless" and not really crimes at all and that it is foolish to legislate morality. Others, sometimes called "moral entrepreneurs," view such morally tinged acts as prostitution, gambling, and drug abuse as harmful and therefore subject to public control. Many public order crimes are sex-related. The internet is a growing area for the distribution of pornographic materials

Paraphilia is the bizarre or abnormal sexual practices that may involve nonhuman objects, humiliation, or children. These acts include frotteurism, voyeurism, exhibitionism, sadomasochism, and pedophilia. Prostitution is another sex-related public order crime. Although prostitution has been practiced for thousands of years and is legal in some areas such as Nevada, most states outlaw commercial sex. There are a variety of prostitutes, including streetwalkers, B-girls, and call girls. A new type of prostitution is cyber prostitution, which is Internet based. Studies indicate that prostitutes come from poor, troubled families and have abusive parents. However, there is little evidence that prostitutes are emotionally disturbed, addicted to drugs, or sexually abnormal. Although prostitution is illegal, some cities (e.g. Amsterdam) have set up adult entertainment areas where commercial sex is tolerated by law enforcement agents.

Pornography involves the sale of sexually explicit material intended to sexually excite paying customers. The depiction of sex and nudity is not illegal, but it does violate the law when it is judged obscene. Obscenity is a legal term that today is defined as material offensive to community standards. Thus, each local jurisdiction must decide what pornographic material is obscene. A growing problem is the exploitation of children in obscene materials (kiddie porn), which has been has expanded through the Internet. The Supreme Court has ruled that local communities can pass statutes outlawing any sexually explicit material. There is no hard evidence that pornography is related to crime or aggression, but data suggest that sexual material with a violent theme is related to sexual violence by those who view it.

Substance abuse is another type of public order crime. Most states and the federal government outlaw a wide variety of drugs they consider harmful, including narcotics, amphetamines, barbiturates, cocaine, hallucinogens, and marijuana. One of the main reasons for the continued ban on drugs is their relationship to crime. Numerous studies have found that drug addicts commit enormous amounts of property and violent crime. Alcohol is another commonly abused substance. Although alcohol is legal to possess, it too has been linked to crime. Drunk driving and deaths caused by drunk drivers are growing national problems. Strategies to control substance abuse range from source control to treatment. Suspected causes of abuse include being part of a lower-class subculture, psychological problems, genetic influences, social learning, problem behavior syndrome, and rational choice. So far, no single method to combat alcohol and drug abuse seems effective. Although legalization is debated, the fact that so many people already take drugs and the association of drug abuse with crime make legalization unlikely in the near term. In the meantime, the government will continue various control approaches such as source control and interdiction strategies as well as community organization and drug education strategies.

CHAPTER OUTLINE

I. Law and Morality

    A. Criminal or Immoral?

    B. Moral Crusaders

    C. Freedom vs. Control

II. Paraphilias

III. Prostitution

    A. Incidence of Prostitution

    B. International Sex Trade

    C. RACE, CULTURE, GENDER AND CRIMINOLOGY: International Trafficking in Prostitution

    D. Types of Prostitutes

        1. Street Walkers

        2. Bar Girls

        3. Brothel Prostitutes

        4. Call Girls

        5. Escort Services/Call Houses

        6. Circuit Travelers

        7. Cyber Prostitute

    E. Becoming a Prostitute

    F. Controlling Prostitution

    G. Legalize Prostitution?

IV. Pornography

    A. Is Pornography Harmful?

    B. Does Pornography Cause Violence?

    C. Pornography and the Law

    D. Can Pornography Be Controlled?

V. Substance Abuse

    A. When Did Drug Use Begin?

    B. Alcohol and Its Prohibition

    C. The Extent of Substance Abuse

    D. The Causes of Substance Abuse

        1. Subculture View

        2. Psychological View

        3. Genetic Factors

        4. Social Learning

        5. Problem Behavior Syndrome

        6. Rational Choice

        7. Is There a Single "Cause" of Drug Abuse?

E. Drugs and Crime

F. PROFILES IN CRIME: A Life in the Drug Trade

G. Drugs and the Law

H. Drug Control Strategies

    1. Interdiction Strategies

    2. Law Enforcement Strategies

    3. Punishment Strategies

    4. Community Strategies

    5. Drug Education and Prevention Strategies

    6. Drug Testing Programs

    7. Treatment Strategies

    8. Employment Programs

I. Legalization of Drugs

CRITICAL THINKING QUESTIONS

1. Find an example of art that some might consider obscene. Write a brief essay explaining your position. Share your idea with the class.

2. Research the negative consequences of prostitution. Present your results to the class.

3. Write an essay that addresses how popular media represents prostitution. How accurate is that portrayal? Could there negative consequences to the media's portrayal?

4. Locate an article about drinking on college campuses. Does it reflect your experiences as a college student? Why or why not?

CHAPTER REVIEW QUESTIONS

Multiple Choice

1. Behavior that is outlawed because it threatens the general well-being of society and challenges its accepted moral principles is called a
    a. public order crime
    b. victimless crime
    c. social norm crime
    d. public order crime.

2. _____ is the erotic interest in members of one's own sex.
    a. Sodomy
    b. Homosexuality
    c. Homophobia
    d. Eroticism

3. A person who creates moral rules, which thus reflect the values of those in power rather than any objective, universal standards of right and wrong is referred to as a
   a. moral rights activist.
   b. moral standard bearer.
   c. moral entrepreneur.
   d. moral leader.

4. Successful moral crusades generally result in _____ that prohibits previously accepted behavior.
   a. civil war
   b. terrorism
   c. public policy change
   d. public discourse

5. The first licensed brothel appeared in _____ in 500 BC.
   a. Greece
   b. Italy
   c. Mesopotamia
   d. Persia

6. Deriving pleasure from receiving pain or inflicting pain is referred to as
   a. frotteurism.
   b. voyeurism.
   c. sadomasochism.
   d. pedophilia.

7. Prostitution legally occurs in _____, but outside large population centers .
   a. California
   b. Florida
   c. Nevada
   d. North Dakota

8. The _____ attempted to end the sale of alcohol in the United States.
   a. Shriners movement
   b. Detoxification entrepreneurs
   c. Temperance movement
   d. Moonshine defense league

9. _____ is the term for material that violates community standards of morality or decency and has no redeeming social value.
   a. Obscene
   b. Sexy
   c. Offensive
   d. Pornographic

10. Lower-class girls who get into prostitution report conflict with _____ before entering "the life."
    a. religious authorities
    b. government policy
    c. friends
    d. school authorities.

11. Immoral acts are considered crimes when they cause
    a. moral outrage.
    b. majority interest.
    c. social harm.
    d. community consensus.

12. Bizarre or abnormal sexual practices that may involve nonhuman objects, humiliation, or children is referred to as
    a. paranormal.
    b. paraphilia.
    c. parapsychological.
    d. parasite.

13. Attaining sexual pleasure through sexual activity with prepubescent children is referred to as
    a. frotteurism.
    b. pedophilia.
    c. voyeurism.
    d. sadomasochism.

14. A _____ is a drug that produces sleep and relieves pain.
    a. stimulant
    b. depressant
    c. narcotic
    d. temperance

15. _____ is the rubbing against or touching a nonconsenting person in a crowd, elevator, or other public area.
    a. Voyeurism
    b. Frotteurism
    c. Pedophilia
    d. Exhibitionism

16. _____ is deriving sexual pleasure from exposing the genitals in order to surprise or shock a stranger.
    a. Voyeurism
    b. Frotteurism
    c. Pedophilia
    d. Exhibitionism

17. At the start of the 1900s, an estimated _____ Americans were opiate users.
    a. 10,000
    b. 100,000
    c. 1,000,000
    d. 10,000,000

18. The aristocrats of prostitution are called
    a. streetwalkers.
    b. B-girls.
    c. brothel prostitutes.
    d. call girls.

19. The newest form of prostitution is called
    a. bar girls.
    b. escort services.
    c. spice girls.
    d. cyber prostitution.

20. Personality testing of known drug users suggests that a significant number of them suffer from
    a. high self-esteem.
    b. psychotic disorders.
    c. low IQ.
    d. poor schools.

21. Why is an exact definition of obscenity so difficult to develop?
    a. Not everyone has the same morality.
    b. Few people have an opinion on the subject.
    c. State laws vary on what judges can enforce.
    d. The Constitution has already defined the term.

22. Mothers Against Drunk Driving is an example of
    a. ethics evangelicals.
    b. moral crusaders.
    c. behavior bohemians.
    d. values vixens.

23. Many objections to homosexual behavior are rooted in
    a. religion.
    b. genetics.
    c. paraphilia.
    d. frotterism.

24. "Streaking" through the campus dining hall is a form of
    a. voyeurism.
    b. pedophilia.
    c. asphyxiophilia.
    d. exhibitionism.

25. _____ are establishments set up for the purposes of prostitution.
    a. Hoochie huts
    b. Brothels
    c. Sexatoriums
    d. Pornodomes

26. An assumed benefit of legalized prostitution would be
    a. fewer "johns."
    b. a more favorable view of prostitution as a career.
    c. reduced public health risks.
    d. a decrease in marriage.

27. _____ was he drive to prohibit the sale of alcohol in the United States, culminating in ratification of the Eighteenth Amendment in 1919.
    a. The Moonshine Maneuver
    b. The Temperance Movement
    c. The Alcohol Crusade
    d. The Boston Beer Party

28. Which of the following TRUE regarding efforts to combat drug abuse?
    a. Drug interdiction strategies have stopped nearly all drugs entering the U.S..
    b. The DARE program has been extremely successful.
    c. No single method to combat alcohol and drug abuse seems effective.
    d. Drug legalization has reduced dependency.

29. Which of the following is NOT a type of prostitute listed in the text?
    a. call girl
    b. skeezer
    c. streetwalker
    d. j-lo

30. Laws against public order are strongly influenced by
    a. public morality.
    b. Roman common law.
    c. the U.S. Constitution.
    d. victimology cases.

True/False

1. T / F To convict a person under the Miller doctrine, the state or local jurisdiction must specifically define obscene conduct in its statute, and the pornographer must engage in that behavior.

2. T / F Material that violates community standards of morality or decency and has no redeeming social value is referred to as obscenity.

3. T / F Prostitution is a transaction with a lot of emotional attachment.

4. T / F The Supreme Court has ruled that no material can be considered obscene.

5. T / F There is great debate whether obscene materials are harmful and are related to violence.

6. T / F More males than females actually engage in prostitution.

7. T / F Women who become prostitutes generally have at least graduated high school.

8. T / F Substance abuse is an ancient practice dating back more than 4,000 years.

9. T / F The Congress passed the Communications Decency Act to combat obscene material on the internet.

10. T / F The Child Sexual Abuse Act makes it illegal to travel abroad in order to engage in child prostitution.

11. T / F Prohibition was very successful in stopping alcohol consumption in the U.S.

12. T / F Genetics are considered the primary cause of substance abuse.

13. T / F There are indications that the DARE program is an overwhelmingly successful.

14. T / F One approach to drug control is to deter the sale and importation of drugs through the systematic apprehension of large volume drug dealers.

15. T / F Advocates of drug legalization contend that if drugs were legalized then distribution could be controlled by government.

Fill in the Blank

1. Because in some criminal acts, such as drug dealing and prostitution, individuals participate willingly, these crime are sometimes called _____.

2. A current moral crusade is to stop female _____ in the Middle East and Africa.

3. The *Lawrence* decision ruled all _____ laws unconstitutional and expanded civil rights for homosexuals.

4. Deriving sexual pleasure from exposing the genitals in order to surprise or shock a stranger is referred to as _____.

5. The earliest record of prostitution appears in ancient _____.

6. Julia Roberts's character in *Pretty Woman* represents a _____.

7. Obtaining sexual pleasure while spying on strangers as they disrobe or engage in sexual behavior is known as _____.

8. Sexually explicit books, magazines, films, or tapes intended to provide sexual titillation and excitement for paying customers are considered _____.

9. Alexa Alberts suggests that _____ prostitution might result in lower rates of HIV.

10. The Monitoring the Future self-reports indicate that _____ percent of all high school seniors reported using an illicit substance.

11. The _____ movement was the drive to prohibit the sale of alcohol in the United States in the early 1900s.

12. Those who view drug abuse as having an environmental basis concentrate on _____ addiction.

13. _____ explains drug/alcohol addiction as one of many problem behaviors.

14. _____ appears to be an important precipitating factor in domestic assault, armed robbery, and homicide cases.

15. _____ focus on severely punishing drug dealers and traffickers.

Essay

1. Discuss the important issue of international trafficking in prostitution.

   - 1 million women
   - Sex tourism in Southeast Asia and Ukraine
   - 50,000 trafficked to the U.S.

2. Discuss the types of prostitutes.

   - Streetwalkers
   - Bar Girls
   - Brothel Prostitutes
   - Call Girls
   - Escort Services/Call Houses
   - Circuit Travelers
   - Cyber Prostitutes

3. Is there a single "cause" of drug abuse?

   - No
   - Lower-class Subculture
   - Psychological problems
   - Genetic influences
   - Social learning
   - Problem Behavior Syndrome
   - Rational Choice

4. Discuss the major drug control strategies that have been developed.

   - Source Control
   - Interdiction Strategies
   - Law enforcement Strategies
   - Punishment Strategies
   - Community Strategies
   - Drug Education and Prevention Strategies
   - Drug-testing Programs
   - Employment Programs

5. Discuss the world historical beginnings of drug abuse and U.S. use.

- Mesopotomia 2,000 BC

- Crusades

- Latin America

- U.S.

    o Heroine addiction (1900)

    o Alcohol Prohibition (1919)

ANSWER KEY FOR CHAPTER REVIEW QUESTIONS

Multiple Choice

1.	(d) public order	p. 311
2.	(b) Homosexuality	p. 314
3.	(c) moral entrepreneur	p. 313
4.	(c) policy change	p. 314
5.	(a) Greece	p. 315
6.	(c) sadomasochism	p. 315
7.	(c) Nevada	p. 318
8.	(c) Temperance	p. 333
9.	(a) Obscenity	p. 328
10.	(d) school authorities	pp. 320-321
11.	(c) social harm	p. 312
12.	(b) paraphilia	p. 314
13.	(b) pedophilia	p. 315
14.	(c) Narcotic	p. 338
15.	(b) Frotteurism	p. 315
16.	(d) Exhibitionism	p. 315
17.	(c) 1,000,000	p. 325
18.	(d) Call girls	p. 319
19.	(d) cyber prostitution	p. 319
20.	(b) psychotic disorder	p. 327
21.	(a) Not everyone has the same morality.	p. 311
22.	(b) moral crusader	pp. 313-314
23.	(a) religion	pp. 311-312
24.	(d) exhibitionism	p. 315
25.	(b) Brothels	pp. 317-318
26.	(c) Reduced public health risks	p. 319
27.	(b) The Temperance Movement	p. 333
28.	(c) no single method seems effective	pp. 335
29.	(d) j-lo	pp. 318-319
30.	(a) public morality	pp. 311-312

True/False

1. True   p. 323
2. True   p. 328
3. False   pp. 315-316
4. False   p. 323
5. True   pp. 321-322
6. False   p. 316
7. False   p. 320
8. True   p. 325
9. True   p. 324
10. True   p. 320
11. False   p. 325
12. False   p. 327
13. True   p. 333
14. True   p. 330
15. True   p. 335

Fill in the Blank

1. victimless   p. 312
2. genital mutilation   p. 313
3. sodomy   p. 314
4. exhibitionism   p. 315
5. Mesopotamia   p. 325
6. streetwalker   p. 318
7. voyeurism   p. 315
8. pornography   p. 321
9. legalizing   p. 321
10. 50   pp. 325-326
11. temperance   p. 333
12. lower-class   p. 327
13. Problem behavior Syndrome   p. 328
14. substance abuse   p. 330
15. Punishment strategies   p. 337

Essay

1. pp. 317-318
2. pp. 318-319
3. pp. 326-328
4. pp. 330-335
5. p. 325

14 The Criminal Justice System

LEARNING OBJECTIVES

After mastering the content of this chapter, a student should be able to:

1. Discuss the history of the criminal justice system.
2. Identify the component agencies of criminal justice.
3. Explain the various stages in the process of justice.
4. Understand how criminal justice is shaped by the rule of law.
5. Explain the elements of the crime control model.
6. Discuss the problem of prisoner reentry.
7. Discuss what is meant by the justice model.
8. Discuss the elements of due process.
9. Argue the merits of the rehabilitation model.
10. Understand the concept of nonintervention.
11. Explain the elements of the restorative justice model.

KEY WORDS AND DEFINITIONS

Criminal justice system - The agencies of government—police, courts, and corrections—responsible for apprehending, adjudicating, sanctioning, and treating criminal offenders. p. 340

Discretion - The use of personal decision making by those carrying out police, judicial, and sanctioning functions within the criminal justice system. p. 342

Community policing – A style of policing that requires departments to reshape their forces into agents of community change. p. 343

Problem-oriented policing – Proactive form of policing: Rather than responding to crime after it occurs, policy identify and respond to potential problems before they occur. p. 343

Landmark decision - A ruling by the U.S. Supreme Court that serves as a precedent for similar legal issues; it often influences the everyday operating procedures of police agencies, trial courts, and corrections institutions. p. 344

Adversary system - U.S. method of criminal adjudication in which prosecution (the state) and defense (the accused) each try to bring forward evidence and arguments, with guilt or innocence ultimately decided by an impartial judge or jury. p. 345

Prosecutor - Public official who represents the government in criminal proceedings, presenting the case against the accused. p. 345

Defendant - In criminal proceedings, the person accused of violating the law. p. 345

Convictability - A case that has a good chance of a conviction. p. 346

Defense attorney - The person responsible for protecting the constitutional rights of the accused and presenting the best possible legal defense; represents a defendant from initial arrest through trial, sentencing, and any appeal. p. 347

Right to counsel - The right of a person accused of crime to have the assistance of a defense attorney in all criminal prosecutions. p. 347

Public defender - An attorney employed by the state whose job is to provide free legal counsel to indigent defendants. p. 347

Pro bono - The provision of free legal counsel to indigent defendants by private attorneys as a service to the profession and the community. p. 347

Probation - The conditional release of a convicted offender into the community under the supervision of a probation officer and subject to certain conditions. p. 348

Incarceration - Confinement in jail or prison. p. 348

Jail - Institution, usually run by the county, for short-term detention of those convicted of misdemeanors and those awaiting trial or other judicial proceedings. p. 348

Prison or penitentiary - State or federally operated facility for the incarceration of felony offenders sentenced by the criminal courts. p. 348

Parole - A conditional early release from prison, with the offender serving the remainder of the sentence in the community under the supervision of a parole officer. p. 349

Arrest - The taking into police custody of an individual suspected of a crime. p. 349

Probable cause - Evidence of a crime, and of a suspect's involvement in it, sufficient to warrant an arrest. p. 349

Booking - Fingerprinting, photographing, and recording personal information of a suspect in police custody. p. 351

Interrogation - The questioning of a suspect in police custody. p. 351

Indictment - A written accusation returned by a grand jury charging an individual with a specified crime, based on the prosecutor's presentation of probable cause. p. 351

Grand jury - A group of citizens chosen to hear testimony in secret and to issue formal criminal accusations (indictments). p. 351

Preliminary hearing - Alternative to a grand jury, in which an impartial lower-court judge decides whether there is probable cause sufficient for a trial. p. 351

Arraignment - The step in the criminal justice process when the accused is brought before the trial judge, formal charges are read, defendants are informed of their rights, a plea is entered, bail is considered, and a trial date is set. p. 351

Bail - A money bond intended to ensure that the accused will return for trial. p. 351

Recognizance - Pledge by the accused to return for trial, which may be accepted in lieu of bail. p. 351

Plea bargain - An agreement between prosecution and defense in which the accused pleads guilty in return for a reduction of charges, a more lenient sentence, or some other consideration. p. 351

Hung jury - A jury that is unable to agree on a decision, thus leaving the case unresolved and open for a possible retrial. p. 351

Disposition - Sentencing of a defendant who has been found guilty; usually involves a fine, probation, or incarceration. p. 351

Appeal - Taking a criminal case to a higher court on the grounds that the defendant was found guilty because of legal error or violation of constitutional rights; a successful appeal may result in a new trial. p. 352

Courtroom work group - Prosecution, defense, and judges working together to resolve criminal cases quickly and efficiently through plea bargaining. p. 355

Law of criminal procedure - Judicial precedents that define and guarantee the rights of criminal defendants and control the various components of the criminal justice system. p. 356

Bill of Rights - The first 10 amendments to the U.S. Constitution, including guarantees against unreasonable search and seizure, self-incrimination, and cruel punishment. p. 356

Crime control model - View that the overriding purpose of the justice system is to protect the public, deter criminal behavior, and incapacitate known criminals; favors speedy, efficient justice and punishment. p. 357

Miranda rights - Rights of criminal defendants, including the right against self-incrimination and right to counsel, spelled out in the case of Miranda v. Arizona. p. 357

Exclusionary rule - The rule that evidence against a defendant may not be presented in court if it was obtained in violation of the defendant's rights. p. 357

Justice model - View that emphasizes fairness and equal treatment in criminal procedures and sentencing. p. 359

Determinate sentencing - Principle that all offenders who commit the same crime should receive the same sentence. p. 360

Due process model - View that focuses on protecting the civil rights of those accused of crime. p. 360

Rehabilitation model - View that sees criminals as victims of social injustice, poverty, and racism and suggests that appropriate treatment can change them into productive, law-abiding citizens. p. 361

Noninterventionist model - The view that arresting and labeling offenders does more harm than good, that youthful offenders in particular should be diverted into informal treatment programs, and that minor offenses should be decriminalized. p. 361

Restorative justice model - View that emphasizes the promotion of a peaceful, just society through reconciliation and reintegration of the offender into society. p. 364

CHAPTER SUMMARY

Criminal justice refers to the formal processes and institutions that have been established to apprehend, try, punish, and treat law violators. The major components of the criminal justice system are the police, the courts, and correctional agencies. Police are the most visible component of the criminal justice system. There are over 17,000 police agencies in the U.S. who are tasked to maintain public order, deter crime, and apprehend law violators. Police departments are now experimenting with community and problem-oriented policing. The courts determine the criminal liability of accused offenders brought before them and dispense sanctions to those found guilty of crime. Corrections agencies provide post-adjudicatory care to offenders who are sentenced by the courts to confinement or community supervision. Dissatisfaction with traditional forms of corrections has spurred the development of community-based facilities and work release and work furlough programs. Justice can also be conceived of as a process through which offenders flow.

There is considerable amount of discretion throughout the criminal justice system. The justice process begins with initial contact by a police agency and proceeds through investigation and custody, trial stages, and correctional system processing (see Figure 14.4). At any stage of the process, the offender may be excused because evidence is lacking, the case is trivial, or a decision maker simply decides to discontinue interest in the case. The bulk of cases are settled before trial in plea bargains with defendants receiving some form of probation -- the conditional release of a convicted offender into the community under the supervision of a probation officer and subject to certain conditions. A portion of more serious offenders will receive jail (misdemeanor offense) or prison sentences (felony offenses).

The U.S. employs the adversary system which is the method of criminal adjudication in which prosecution (the state) and defense (the accused) each try to bring forward evidence and arguments, with guilt or innocence ultimately decided by an impartial judge or jury. The procedures, policies, and practices employed within the criminal justice system are scrutinized by the courts to make sure they do not violate the guidelines in the first 10 amendments to the U.S. Constitution. If a violation occurs, the defendant can appeal the case and seek to overturn the conviction. The Supreme Court of the United States is the highest court in the land. Among the rights that must be honored are freedom from illegal searches and seizures and treatment with overall fairness and due process.

Several different philosophies or perspectives dominate the justice process (see Figure 14.9). The crime control model asserts that the goals of justice are protection of the public and incapacitation of known offenders. The justice model calls for fair, equal treatment for all offenders. The due process model emphasizes liberal principles, such as legal rights and procedural fairness for the offender. The rehabilitation model views the justice system as a wise and caring parent. The noninterventionist perspective calls for minimal interference in offenders' lives. The restorative justice model seeks non-punitive, humane solutions to the conflict inherent in crime and victimization. Current the crime control and justice models currently dominate the criminal justice system.

CHAPTER OUTLINE

I. What Is the Criminal Justice System?
    A. Police and Law Enforcement
    B. PROFILES IN CRIME: Mafia Cops
    C. The Criminal Court System
        1. Court Structure
        2. The Supreme Court
        3. Prosecution and Defense
        4. Criminal Prosecution
            a) Prosecutor
            b) Defendant
            c) Convictability
        5. Criminal Defense
            a) Defense Attorney
                (1) Protecting constitutional rights of defendants
                (2) Presenting best possible legal defense
            b) Right to Counsel
            c) Pro bono
    D. Corrections
        1. probation
        2. jail
        3. prison (penitentiary)
        4. truth in sentencing
        5. parole
II. The Process of Justice
    A. Decision Points
        1. Initial Contact
        2. Investigation
        3. Arrest
        4. Custody
        5. Complaint/Charging
        6. Preliminary Hearing/Grand Jury
            a) Indictment
            b) Information
        7. Arraignment
        8. Bail or detention
        9. Plea Bargaining
        10. Adjudication
        11. Disposition

CRITICAL THINKING QUESTIONS

1. If you were to be a member of the criminal justice system, which would it be? Why?

2. List the first ten Amendments to the U.S. Constitution. Which apply directly to the criminal justice system? How?

3. Read about an arrest in your local area. Decide what type and level of bail you would require of the suspect. Does it match the actual result?

4. Do you consider the recent hanging of Saddam Hussein to be cruel and inhuman? Why? Is there an alternative punishment you would have recommended?

CHAPTER REVIEW QUESTIONS

Multiple Choice

1. Approximately _____ law enforcement agencies operate in the United States.
   a. 10,000
   b. 13,000
   c. 17,000
   d. 20,000

2. While firmly entrenched in our culture, the common criminal justice agencies have existed for only _____ years or so.
   a. 350
   b. 300
   c. 250
   d. 150

3. The agencies of the criminal justice system include
   a. police.
   b. private security.
   c. posses.
   d. vigilantes.

4. Law enforcement agencies have been charged with
   a. deterring lawful behavior.
   b. keeping the peace.
   c. humiliating potential criminals.
   d. creating laws.

5. In recent years, police departments have experimented with new forms of law enforcement, including
   a. task force control.
   b. community policing.
   c. SWAT.
   d. martial law.

6. Each year, _____ citizens have contact with the police.
   a. 45,000,000
   b. 3,200,000
   c. 210,000
   d. 17,000

7. The _____ are considered by many to be the core element in the administration of criminal justice.
   a. judges
   b. police
   c. criminal courts
   d. prosecutors

8. Most states employ a/an _____ court system.
   a. unitiered
   b. bitiered
   c. multitiered
   d. independent

9. Lower courts
   a. try felony cases.
   b. try misdemeanors.
   c. review the criminal procedures of trial courts.
   d. Review Supreme Court decisions.

10. The U.S. Supreme Court issues a _____ when it calls for the transcripts of a case proceeding for review.
    a. cart blanch
    b. magna carta
    c. writ of certiorari
    d. carta magnus

11. Which courts are the trial courts of the federal system?
    a. U.S. district courts
    b. Intermediate federal courts of appeals
    c. The U.S. Supreme Court
    d. Federal Traffic Courts

12. Prosecutors bring forth cases with a high
    a. appealability.
    b. durability.
    c. convictability.
    d. overturnability.

13. The United States utilizes a _____ adjudication system where prosecution and defense each bring forth evidence and argument.
    a. dictatorial
    b. conflictual
    c. prosecutorial
    d. adversary

14. The court system has long provided counsel to the indigent on the basis of the _____ Amendment of the U.S. Constitution.
    a. First
    b. Fourth
    c. Fifth
    d. Sixth

15. _____ hold the most dangerous inmates.
    a. Half-way houses
    b. Minimum-security prisons
    c. Medium-security prisons
    d. Maximum-security prisons

16. The most common correctional treatment is
    a. incarceration.
    b. probation.
    c. incapacitation.
    d. parole.

17. The provision of free legal counsel to indigent defendants by private attorneys as a service to the profession and the community is called
    a. magna carta.
    b. pro bono.
    c. legal welfare.
    d. poverty prosecution.

18. In about half the states and in the federal system, the decision to bring a suspect to trial is made by a group of citizens brought together to form a/an
    a. preliminary hearing.
    b. federal jury.
    c. indictment hearing.
    d. grand jury.

19. _____ brings the accused before the court that will actually try the case.
    a. Arraignment
    b. Disposition
    c. Adjudication
    d. Investigation

20. The _____ makes protecting the public the top priority of the criminal justice system.
    a. crime control model
    b. justice model
    c. due process model
    d. non-intervention model

21. The criminal justice system is responsible for _____ criminal offenders.
    a. compromising
    b. adjudicating
    c. mocking
    d. devastating

22. When an inmate is so dangerous that he is a constant threat to guards and other inmates, he is sent to a _____ security prison such as Pelican Bay.
    a. minimum
    b. medium
    c. maximum
    d. boot camp

23. The vast majority of criminal court cases result in
    a. parole.
    b. plea bargains.
    c. trial.
    d. dismissal.

24. "Judge Judy" was a _____ where she handled felony cases before her television career.
    a. meter maid
    b. parole officer
    c. superior court judge
    d. lower court judge

25. There are approximately _____ sworn police officers in the United States.
    a. 250,000
    b. 500,000
    c. 750,000
    d. 1,000,000

26. _____ is a style of policing that requires departments to become agents of social change at work directly with citizens to reduce crime and disorder.
    a. Community policing
    b. Aggressive policing
    c. Tactical policing
    d. Parole Policing

27. You have just been conditional released from prison and will complete the rest of your sentence under government supervision. You are on
    a. probation.
    b. probable cause.
    c. parole.
    d. arrest review.

28. Which of the following is TRUE regarding the criminal justice system?
    a. There are very few people involved in the process.
    b. The justice system is bound by the rule of law.
    c. Most cases are handled similarly to the O.J. Simpson or Scott Peterson case.
    d. Constitutional protections apply only at the federal and not state level.

29. The statement of "You have the right to remain silent..." is known as
    a. Valor verdict.
    b. Davis decree.
    c. Exclusionary rules.
    d. Miranda rights.

30. Which of the following factors seems to create the greatest stress on the courts?
    a. A lack of defendants.
    b. The lack of established court rules.
    c. Too few prison cells for the accused.
    d. The very high caseload.

True/False

1. T / F Prisons hold those convicted of misdemeanors and those awaiting trial or those involved in other proceedings, such as grand jury deliberation, arraignments, or preliminary hearings.

2. T / F The first 10 Amendments to the U.S. Constitution, ratified in 1791, are generally called the Bill of Rights.

3. T / F The crime control model is rooted in the social learning theory.

4. T / F According to the justice model, it is futile to rehabilitate criminals.

5. T / F Crime control advocates see themselves as protectors of civil rights.

6. T / F The due process model embraces the notion that some constitutional rights can be ignored if it means protecting law-abiding citizens.

7. T / F The nonintervention model calls for limiting government intrusion into the lives of people, especially minors, who run afoul of the law.

8. T / F The vast majority of convicted felons receive probation.

9. T / F Research on sentencing has failed to show a definitive pattern of racial discrimination.

10. T / F Mediation is a focus of the noninterventionist model.

11. T / F Most criminal cases are resolved through plea bargaining.

12. T / F Determinant sentencing seeks to tailor criminal sentences to fit each defendant.

13. T / F Most arrestees, even felons, are released on their own recognizance.

14. T / F Hung juries result when a jury chooses a death penalty sentence for murderers.

15. T / F Advocates of the restorative justice model say that state efforts to punish and control reduce crime.

Fill in the Blank

1. _____ handle most indigent legal defense.

2. The most common correctional treatment is _____.

3. Another name for the _____ hearing is a probable cause hearing.

4. _____ requires inmates to serve a greater amount of their sentence behind bars before being eligible for parole.

5. The crime control philosophy emphasizes protecting society and compensating _____.

6. _____ usually involves a fine, community service, a period of incarceration, or some combination of these penalties.

7. A _____ decision is a ruling by the U.S. Supreme Court that serves as a precedent for similar legal issues.

8. _____ is the conditional early release from prison.

9. _____ is evidence of a crime, and of a suspect's involvement in it, sufficient to warrant an arrest.

10. _____ is the questioning of a suspect in police custody.

11. A group of citizens chosen to hear testimony in secret and to issue formal criminal accusations (indictments) is called _____.

12. A money bond intended to ensure that the accused will return for trial is called _____.

13. When the prosecutor, defense attorney, and judge work together to resolve criminal cases quickly and efficiently through plea bargaining, the group is called _____.

14. The _____ is the judicial precedents that define and guarantee the rights of criminal defendants and control the various components of the criminal justice system.

15. The _____ model focuses on protecting the civil rights of those accused of crime.

Essay

1. Discuss the important elements of the criminal court system.

    - Court structure

    - The Supreme Court

    - Prosecution and Defense

    - Criminal Prosecution

    - Criminal Defense

2. Briefly discuss the different types of case dispositions.

    - Fine

    - Probation

    - Jail/Prison

    - Death Penalty

    - Parole

3. Discuss the importance of custody in the criminal justice process.

    - Fingerprinting

    - Photograph

    - Lineup

    - Interrogation

4. Explain what is a "landmark" Supreme Court decision and provide and example.

    - Precedent

    - *Gideon v. Wainwright*

    - *Powell v. Alabama*

    - *Argersinger v. Hamlin*

5. Briefly describe the two major "impediments" to effectiveness of the crime control model.

    - Miranda Rights

    - Exclusionary Rule

ANSWER KEY FOR CHAPTER REVIEW QUESTIONS

Multiple Choice

1.	(c) 17,000	p. 341
2.	(d) 150	p. 340
3.	(a) police	p. 341
4.	(b) keeping the peace	p. 342
5.	(c) community policing	p. 343
6.	(a) 45,000,000	p. 342
7.	(c) criminal courts	p. 343
8.	(c) multitiered	p. 344
9.	(b) try misdemeanors	p. 344
10.	(c) writ of certiorari	p. 344
11.	(a) U.S. district courts	p. 344
12.	(c) convictability	p. 346
13.	(d) adversary	p. 345
14.	(d) Sixth	p. 347
15.	(d) Maximum security prisons	p. 348
16.	(b) probation	p. 348
17.	(b) pro bono	p. 347
18.	(d) grand jury	p. 351
19.	(a) Arraignment	p. 351
20.	(a) crime control model	p. 357
21.	(b) adjudicating	p. 351
22.	(c) maximum	p. 348
23.	(b) plea bargains	p. 351
24.	(c) superior court	p. 345
25.	(d) 1,000,000	p. 340
26.	(a) Community policing	p. 343
27.	(c) parole	p. 349
28.	(b) The justice system is bound by the rule of law.	p. 347
29.	(d) Miranda rights	p. 357
30.	(d) The very high caseload,	pp. 345-346

True/False

1.	False	p. 348
2.	True	p. 356
3.	False	p. 357
4.	True	p. 359
5.	False	p. 357
6.	False	p. 360
7.	True	pp. 361-362
8.	False	p. 343
9.	True	p. 362
10.	True	pp. 363-364
11.	True	p. 355
12.	False	p. 360

13. True pp. 351-352
14. False p. 351
15. False p. 364

Fill in the Blank

1. Public defenders p. 347
2. probation p. 348
3. preliminary p. 351
4. Truth-in-sentencing p. 348
5. victims pp. 357-358
6. Disposition pp. 351-352
7. landmark p. 344
8. Parole pp. 349-350
9. Probable cause pp. 349-350
10. Interrogation p. 351
11. grand jury p. 351
12. bail p. 351
13. courtroom work group pp. 355-356
14. law of criminal procedure p. 356
15. due process p. 370

Essay

1. pp. 343-348
2. p. 352
3. pp. 350-351
4. pp. 344-347
5. pp. 357-358